One of the earliest extant "commentaries" on the Acts of the Apostles is the collection of homilies preached by John Chrysostom, bishop of Constantinople in 400 C.E. In this first volume in the *Preaching the Word* series, Bill Shiell is situated in this long-standing tradition of plumbing Acts for its homiletical insights. Shiell's attention to the rhetorical shape and social setting of this "foundational document" for early Christianity produces a theological treasure trove. *Acts* joins that very small group of commentaries capable of informing seasoned scholars and, at the same time, edifying the person in the pew, seeking to become a more faithful follower of the Way.

— Mikeal C. Parsons
Professor and Macon Chair in Religion
Baylor University

Dr. Shiell proves to Bible readers, preachers, and scholars that commentaries do not have to be dry and devoid of application. Many commentaries lead us down a winding and sometimes confusing scholastic path, but *Acts* blends the best of scholarship with practical insight to masterfully guide us through the grand story of the early Church. Dr. Shiell's excellently written text is seasoned with dynamic narrative and accessible context in order to aid students of God's word to gain a deeper understanding of early Christianity. I highly recommend adding the *Preaching the Word* series to your sermon preparation, Bible study, or personal library.

—Rev. Alan Rudnick
Executive Minister
DeWitt Community Church in DeWitt, NY

When academics presume to tell pastors how to preach a text, the pastoral context goes missing; when pastors examine the texts of Scripture the academic research is often ignored. But when an academic is also a pastor and when the pastor is an academic, the two—text and church—can be brought together in a way that floods a serious grappling with the text with pastoral theology. Which is exactly what William Shiell, now President of Northern Seminary, accomplishes in this rich and textured new approach to preaching one of the New Testament's great books—The Acts of the Apostles. This will be a mine for pastors for decades.

—Scot McKnight
Julius R. Mantey Professor of New Testament
Northern Seminary

Smyth & Helwys Publishing, Inc.
6316 Peake Road
Macon, Georgia 31210-3960
1-800-747-3016
©2017 by William D. Shiell
All rights reserved.

Library of Congress Cataloging-in-Publication Data

Shiell, William David, 1972- author.-
Acts
by William D. Shiell.
Macon : Smyth & Helwys, 2017.
Series: Preaching the word |
Includes bibliographical references.
LCCN 2016056024
ISBN 9781573129060 (pbk. : alk. paper)
LCSH: Bible. Acts--Commentaries.
LCC BS2625.53 .S55 2017
DDC 226.6/07--dc23

2016056024

Disclaimer of Liability: With respect to statements of opinion or fact available in this work of nonfiction, Smyth & Helwys Publishing Inc. nor any of its employees, makes any warranty, express or implied, or assumes any legal liability or responsibility for the accuracy or completeness of any information disclosed, or represents that its use would not infringe privately-owned rights.

Acts

William D. Shiell

Also by William D. Shiell

Ezekiel Annual Bible Study: God's Presence in Performance

Sessions with Matthew

Dedication

For my Professors:

Mikeal C. Parsons

Naymond Keathley

Charles Talbert

William H. Bellinger

Heidi J. Hornik

Brian L. Harbour

J. Bradley Creed

J. Randall O'Brien

Dennis Sansom

Bill J. Leonard

In Memoriam

Ruth Ann Foster

A.J. "Chip" Conyers

Contents

Part Three: Challenge of the Gospel

Preface

The book of Acts is a charter document for congregations who love the resurrected Jesus. Luke writes how the gospel spread "unhindered" from Jerusalem to Judea, Samaria, and Rome, as well as to communities in between. Beginning with a group of disciples in the upstairs room, Luke takes us on an adventure of faith that changes cities and challenges lives through the power of the Spirit and the work of the church. Some of the main characters are its earliest converts. Saul turns from persecutor to proclaimer. Some of the officials become foils for the spread of the word. Women and men serve, proclaim, and share together.

I have divided Acts into three sections. Each one reflects the theme of the book and the scope of the work that Luke addresses. Part 1 is entitled Charter for a Common Way (1–12). Beginning with Jesus' ascension, the disciples learn how to form a resurrection community and offer a pattern that shapes Christian thinking for generations. This section is not an instruction manual but a guide for the character formation of believers to learn, follow, and grow together.

Part 2 is Change in the Cities (13–20). The resurrection of Jesus and the power of the Spirit disrupt cities across the Mediterranean region. As apostles such as Paul, Timothy, Priscilla, and others arrive on assignment, they discover that these cities are changing because of the impact of the church. The church is even accused of "turning the world upside down" in Thessalonica.

Part 3 is the Challenge of the Gospel (21–28). Turning toward Rome, we discover that Paul challenges the Roman and Jerusalem leadership with his messages. Likewise, the gospel challenges us as it crosses boundaries and changes lives.

This book began in a New Testament rhetorical criticism seminar in 2001 at Baylor University with Dr. Mikeal C. Parsons. The research for this book is largely a product of the insights gleaned from that class, his commentary on *Acts* in the Paideia series, and Kavin Rowe's insights from his book *World Upside Down*. As I've written these sermons, I've had the privilege of seeing congregations respond firsthand to this work, and I'm grateful to First Baptist Churches of Knoxville and Tallahassee for their influence on these messages. Several editors and friends have read and offered feedback along the way. Thank you to Keith Gammons and the team at Smyth & Helwys for inviting me to participate in this series. My deepest thanks go to Jared Coleman, Andrew Gardner, and Amy Parks, who have offered great insight as editors. The pastoral staff of First Baptist Church of Tallahassee, Florida, especially Josh Hall, helped me develop the theme of the "common" issues in the first section of the book. We used several of these sermons to launch a ministry called "Life Groups." I first preached most of these sermons and Bible studies on Sunday mornings and Wednesday evenings at First Baptist Church of Tallahassee, Florida. Their feedback, questions, and comments have offered me immeasurable assistance.

As always, I am so grateful to my wife, Kelly, my partner in ministry who encourages me to live out my calling for the local church and now with our new friends at Northern Seminary. My sons Parker and Drake are a constant encouragement and support along the journey. I dedicate this book to my professors at Samford University and Baylor University, scholars who taught this Theophilus to love the resurrected Jesus with all of my mind.

Part One

Charter for a Common Way

Before we called ourselves "Christians," we were known as the Way. We were a sect of Judaism known for following a risen Messiah named Jesus. We gathered in synagogues and houses. We shared possessions and sent missionaries. The first section of Acts (chapters 1–12) describes our beginnings.

Growing out of the soil of first-century Judaism, the early followers of the Way held several core things in common. If you read through Acts 1–12, you notice that it reads like a charter document for a new organization forming in the community. But this is not your average non-profit or small business venture. This is the work of God that is only made possible because of nine characteristics. Each one is something these people have in common. The Greek word for this group is *koine*. It's the root for our words "communication" and "company." Sometimes we call it "fellowship," but it was so much more. They held these things in common:

1. Person of Jesus Christ (Acts 1:1-25). The risen and exalted Jesus bound them together. He became their parent and example for these brothers and sisters who were moving throughout the world.

2. Power from the Holy Spirit (Acts 2). When they came together, the whole place was shaken. Fire fell. Wind blew. It was just a sign to them that they could not do this on their own. God had to work, and God worked through the third person of the Trinity, the

Holy Spirit. The followers of the Way testified in awe, wonder, and amazement.

3. Persistent people from all phases of life (Acts 2:41–3:10). They welcomed and involved everyone, including non-Jewish ethnicities and the mentally and physically disabled. They networked throughout Jerusalem and communicated their message. Women and men were filled with the Spirit and proclaimed the message as they were gifted.

4. Promise of Jesus' imminent return (Acts 3:11–4:21). They knew that the end was near and they lived like it. Doing so gave them a sense of hopeful urgency to share their faith and change their lives.

5. Provisions submitted to someone else's authority (Acts 4:22–5:11). They placed their possessions and property at the apostles' feet so they could use these resources to extend their communal life to others.

6. Place of work and life (Acts 5:12-42). They committed themselves to a neighborhood and a workplace, which were often one and the same. There they shared a meal, much like a potluck dinner, and provided for each other.

7. Performance of the message (Acts 6:1–8:3). Through people like Stephen and others, they proclaimed a common core set of beliefs that was the fabric of their community. They shared testimony of the gospel and people responded.

8. Pursuit of common interests (Acts 8:4–9:31). Our word for "pursuit" comes from the same Greek word we might use to describe a hot or cold thermos. The temperature depends on the contents of the container. The church grew very passionate about their pursuit to demonstrate God's reign in Jesus Christ to the world. Most of the time they did this through service.

9. Pressure from insiders and outsiders (Acts 12:1-25). Suffering was part of the journey. Sometimes they felt pain because they felt resistance, even violence, from opponents. Many times they simply suffered because that's the way life is. Other times they faced internal conflicts. They learned to use all of it.

At First Baptist Tallahassee, I used these messages to prepare our church for a ministry called "Life Groups," which consists of intentional small groups with an outward focus. Patterned after the groups in Acts 1–12, Life Groups were designed to reach the unreached, unchurched, and un-involved.

Many of these sermons are comparison and contrast messages that use the rhetorical technique called *synkrisis*. These sermons invite congregations to compare their image of the risen Christ to the picture of Jesus they were taught as a child, to differentiate between groups that gather in a temple or building versus those that meet in a house, to note the differences between groups that are open and those that are closed. By comparing our lives to those of the characters in Acts, we are better able to see how we match up with the character and impact of the Way. We evaluate our ministries today against its message, and we learn to follow the One who sent us to "the uttermost parts of the earth" (Acts 1:8, New English Bible).

1

Where Do We Go from Here?

Acts 1:1–8

Frederick Buechner said that vocation is the place where our deepest longing and the world's greatest need intersect.[1] For Christians, God's greatest challenge greets us at this intersection. He calls us to a place we would not go, had it not been for a change in our lives.

This is where we find the disciples on the top of the Mount of Olives. Here Jesus met with them, prayed over the city of Jerusalem, rode a donkey, and then departed. His ascension called, changed, and empowered them.

Jesus could have stayed on earth, presumably living forever, but the Gospels and the New Testament do not suggest that was really ever an option. The ascension is the doctrinal centerpiece for Jesus' departure and coronation. It describes his move from earthly Savior to heavenly King. Resurrection validates his earthly life and confirms his identity as the Son of God. Ascension crowns him as Lord of All and inaugurates his reign in heaven as it is already revealed on earth.

A Beginning Exit

Luke ends his biography of Jesus' life with his ascension. Acts opens like a sequel, reprising the ending of Luke's Gospel. In Acts, the opening begins with an exit. The disciples gather and listen, and suddenly Jesus disappears into heaven. The metaphor of a journey was commonly used in the ancient world for authority figures the way it is used today. When a president or king moves to higher office, we say the leader is "going up" to Washington or London.

We know heaven is not spatially in the sky any more than it's just beyond the locked door. The cloud image is not so much a taxi service to heaven as it is a way of depicting something that no words can describe. The point of the passage is not to display the path to eternity. Rather, it depicts the coronation of the King and promises his return.

Jesus ascends to the place of authority, seated on the throne of heaven and earth. Jesus is God, God is going up, and God is in charge. We had better be prepared for Jesus' return. The ascension is necessary because Jesus cannot do the work that he was sent to do without his departure. The disciples know Jesus' presence throughout the book of Acts. They share his name as they journey. However, the focus of Acts is not about how Jesus goes to his throne but about how the disciples respond to his departure. That's why they gather, discern, pray, and discuss leadership.

Following an Ascended Leader

This model of leadership and education is so different from the predominant form in our world. When there is a problem in the corporate, athletic, education, or political worlds, our society defaults by blaming whoever is on top. The leader is replaced. If we want to fix the city, we change the mayor; if we want to fix the office, we replace the CEO; if we want to fix the athletic team, we need a new coach.

Today's education focuses on training and information. If we know the facts and master the core competencies, presumably we then are equipped to function in a job.

Christian leadership and formation are much different. They begin with love for God (Theophilus). Leadership does not change from the top down. The disciples change from the inside out. They love Jesus and worship him as Lord. Jesus remains in charge, and the disciples respond by becoming the community that Christ wants them to be. Education and formation are not focused on mastering a set of facts. Even Jesus does not explain everything they need to know prior to his departure. They could not bear to know it anyway. Education comes through love, discipleship, mentoring, and on-the-job experience. Their lives and behavior reflect as much (or more) of their observations about Jesus as the information he provided.

The disciples learn their roles like a group of siblings who have discovered that they share the same parent. They must learn how to work together while facing enormous challenges; the only way to learn is to experience life together. They must choose to trust each other and follow Christ through the journey.

The disciples realize that they must choose to become the disciples that Christ has equipped them to be. They will never know enough, but they can choose to move forward. That's the step Jesus asks them to take. He wants them to be prepared to go to four places: Jerusalem, Judea, Samaria, and the uttermost parts of the earth. Jesus calls us to go to these places figuratively in our world as well.

Discovering Where Jesus Sends Us

Eric Swanson suggests four different places that represent the Location and People outlined in Acts 1:8 (see chart below).

Jerusalem: These are the people closest to you in location as well as in values and belief systems. These people are similar to you but still need your help. They are your neighbors, friends, church members, and those you know and love. Your Jerusalem could even be the place you work.

Judea: This experience requires you to travel some distance, but the people there are probably still very much like you. Your Judea may be a mission trip with other Christians, a place where God is calling you to serve, or a vacation spot with friends and families.

Samaria: These are the people who are very different from you, but who still live close by. They are not the people in your neighborhood. They live across the tracks, or downtown, or at the homeless shelter. They are outside of your comfort zone, but can still be found right around here.

Earth: A place that requires travel across the country or ocean.

We will never know enough. In fact, we can spend as much time as we want studying, brushing up, and thinking through what we need to do. But we are still commanded to do something. As William Willimon says:

> Even to know all *about* Jesus (and to know Jesus), even to have received instruction from Jesus himself for forty days is not enough to accomplish the church's mission. The challenge is not the intellectual one of

knowing enough to tell about Jesus but rather the challenge is to have the authorization and empowerment which enable succeeding witnesses to be *doing* the work of Jesus. Until those who know the facts also experience the power, they do well first to wait in Jerusalem to pray.[2]

When my older son, Parker, was four years old, he and I flew to Kentucky to meet our family for a wedding. We lived in San Angelo, Texas, and drove four hours to fly out of Dallas/Fort Worth. Prior to the trip, Parker asked me a very important question, "Daddy, is my plane going to be a big plane or a *little*, tiny plane? I don't want to go on a big plane; I want to go on a little, tiny plane."

I assured him (as any good father would do) that we would ask the pilot when we got there if we could have a little, tiny plane. Parker knew better than to believe his dad, so he took the issue up with his mother.

"Mommy," he said, "I don't want to ride on a big plane; I want to ride on a little, tiny plane."

He did not let it drop. All the way to Dallas, he insisted on flying on a small plane. When we checked in and arrived at the gate, of course, the plane was a huge jet. I practically had to drag him onto the plane.

When we were buckled in, I told him that we would be going fast but if he looked out the window, everything would be fine. He said, "Daddy would you hold my hand while we go on the runway?" The protests continued: "Daddy, I don't want to go on the runway; I don't want to go real fast; I don't want to go on the big plane."

Just as the plane lifted off the runway, Parker saw that everything was fine. He looked at me with his big green eyes and said, "I like being on a big plane, Daddy." Five minutes later he said, "Daddy, I don't need you to hold my hand anymore."

In order for Parker to learn to fly, we had to get on the plane and take off. I could not share any more information. We just had to go from that place to our next destination. So Jesus ascends, and we go.

Where Is God Calling You?

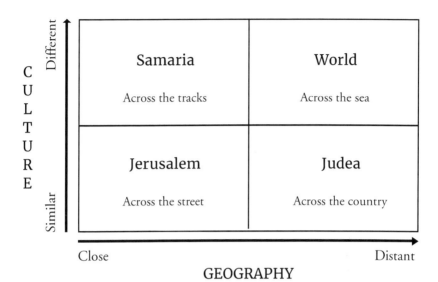

Table 1. Where is God Calling You?[3]

Notes

1. Frederick Buechner, *Beyond Words: Daily Readings in the ABC's of Faith* (New York: HarperOne, 2004), 404.

2. William Willimon, *Acts*, Interpretation (Louisville: John Knox Press, 1988), 21.

3. Adapted from Eric Swanson and Rick Rusaw, *The Externally Focused Quest: Becoming the Best Church for the Community* (San Francisco: Josey-Bass, 2010), 90.

Christ Changes Community

Acts 1:9–26

A sermon for Graduate Recognition Day

If the ascension was Jesus' coronation day, it was the disciples' graduation day. As we learned in the previous message, Jesus provided enough information for them to begin the journey, but they would have to trust in the reigning Christ to guide them. No longer would they have Jesus around every day to lead them; instead, he took off so they could go out. They returned to the classroom—the upper room—to wait for further instructions, just as Jesus told them to do. And while they waited and prayed, Peter stood up and gave the commencement address of his life.

Discipleship Commencement

Notice in the text, on the Mount of Olives, just across from Jerusalem, Jesus ascends with instructions. The disciples stand around, gazing into heaven, and he sends them back to their homeroom—the upstairs room—to wait. He said he would return. He promised it; now they must wait. The same place where Jesus shared his last meal with them is home base where Jesus will meet them.

Assembled now is a group that has grown not only in composition but also in structure. Mary, Jesus' mother, is a disciple. First, there were 12, then a band of 70 to go out into the neighborhoods. Now they are large enough to have a prayer meeting. In Jewish tradition, a prayer circle consisted of 120. (Ironically, this is also the size of the Sanhedrin that sentenced Jesus to die.) So now, gathered together in this upstairs room with a large enough community around them, they prayed, and someone found his voice and stood up.

He had been the one who denied Jesus, but in the midst of denial, Jesus turned back and looked at Peter (Luke 22:61). Those eyes seemed to burn a hole right into his heart. And as they waited for the Spirit to show up at Pentecost, there in the upper room, their classroom, they prayed.

Can you imagine going back to homeroom, or around the flagpole, to wait and pray? That is precisely what the disciples do. They wait.

I imagine that in that room, the disciples were staring at each other because one person, who did not ascend, was missing. One of their own had betrayed Jesus and committed suicide. That person was Judas. In fact he had a "share" in discipleship, a word also meaning "lot" or inheritance. The Greek word for "share" is also our word for "clergy"—*cleros*.[1]

Judas took the money that the Jewish leaders paid him for his betrayal of Jesus and bought a field with it. In the process of apostasy, he was actually buying his own cemetery. In the Vietnam War, soldiers who died in battle were said to have "bought the farm." That is, they finally made it home.[2] Some farmers even took a life insurance policy out so that when they died, the estate would be paid off. When they died, they "bought the farm." Judas bought the farm literally and died in it.

The only person who could address this issue was someone who knew how close he came to being Judas. And that was Peter. He was supposed to be the class president. He was always speaking before everyone else could. But that final night, he was caught in the scandal of his life: he denied Jesus. Now, with courage, faith, and prayer, he stood up and preached. As he does, Peter reminds all of us graduates from the school of discipleship something very important that he'd learned and that we need to learn today: *Christ works in the chaos of our lives.*

Christ Works in the Chaos

Life is random and chaotic. Friends die. Parents suffer. Grandparents buy farms. Children move away. People disappoint us. And most of it causes us to wait longer than we expected to do what we thought we planned.

Life is also very wonderful and beautiful and good. There are incredibly great people that you meet along life's journey. Many of them surround you with incredible and rare kinds of love, and most of them you do not recognize until after they are gone. You look back and you see the work that they have done for you and through you. We serve a God in Jesus Christ who, through the power of his ascension, makes it possible for you to trust him in the times when people disappoint you, when your plans go awry, when your relationships fail, when someone betrays you. Trusting Christ gives us time to wait.

You are emerging at an incredibly great time—one of those times I would love to experience in your shoes right now. The tide is going out on Christendom, so people of faith are recovering vibrancy and choice. It is not easy to simply choose to be a Christian.

In a multigenerational church, you have also been given a great foundation of life and faith. Trust the foundation you have been given. What no church can prepare and train you for is the randomness of life: tornadoes, hurricanes, death, joy, and celebration. Life is full of surprises, both good and bad.

One of the most surprising things about the lives of the earliest disciples is that they do not hide from surprises; they use them. And they *turn to the Psalms to navigate the chaos.*

The Psalms Help Us Navigate the Chaos

Peter cites two psalms in this text. Psalm 69:25 explains that Judas was part of God's plan. Psalm 109:8 explains the importance of moving on and choosing a successor. Now what does that tell us? I would suggest to you that this is the way the disciples manage—and perhaps how we should manage—the chaos, disappointments, and struggles of life. They pray through psalms.

For this group of 120 believers gathered in the upper room, Psalms is their prayer book. Why? Bonhoeffer explains in a little book called *Life Together* that the Psalter was Christ's prayer book. Psalms points them to Christ, they see Christ's words in psalms, and psalms become the way that Christ speaks to them. The psalms are, as Bonhoeffer puts it, "the vicarious prayer of Christ for his church…Jesus Christ prays through the Psalter to his congregation."[3]

Through praying the psalms, Jesus shows his followers how to trust the people that God has assembled in their life. The only way they can move forward is to be together. Christ has equipped them with a community now and with a community to come that will guide and sustain them. This is their little "band of brothers," a group of friends who will guide, comfort, and console each other through the struggles ahead.[4] They cannot go it alone. In fact they will not go it alone, and they will always have a group that will do this together with them.

Shakespeare uses this phrase "band of brothers" in *Henry V* (Act 4, Scene 3). Prior to the battle of Agincourt, on the eve of St. Crispin's Day, the king assembles his outnumbered troops for battle. They have a secret weapon—the longbow—but they will need to trust each other to use it. He calls their names, as if he is calling roll, and then uses this phrase to unite them into one group, reflecting our scene in Acts 1.

> Harry the King, Bedford and Exeter,
> Warwick and Talbot, Salisbury and Gloucester,
> Be in their flowing cups freshly remember'd.
> This story shall the good man teach his son;
> And Crispin Crispian shall ne'er go by,
> From this day to the ending of the world,
> But we in it shall be remember'd;
> We few, we happy few, we band of brothers;
> For he to-day that sheds his blood with me
> Shall be my brother; be he ne'er so vile,
> This day shall gentle his condition;
> And gentlemen in England now a-bed
> Shall think themselves accursed they were not here,
> And hold their manhoods cheap whiles any speaks
> That fought with us upon Saint Crispin's day.

Now obviously, this is no battle against the French, but the book of Acts calls their names nonetheless. It is a community list, not a roll call for war. The German evangelicals called this kind of community *gemeinschaft*. It is the complete life of togetherness. It's the sense that we will eat, pray, worship, share, and do life as a community. When we are together, we pray psalms. Bonhoeffer suggests three steps:

1. Read psalms as if Christ is praying for you.

2. Pray the words with others. Read them in community. Ask different people to say the words.

3. Use their words when times of trial come to pray to God. They give us words to say that we would not normally say, especially at church.[5]

God Calls New People to Share Community

As you do, God not only directs, but *calls new people to share the community.* He prepares them to realize how much they are going to need each other. They realize that Christ has already placed people *in* the community to fill the void left by Judas: Justus and Matthias. In order to choose, they pray in community, and then employ the seemingly random method of casting lots. It is that word *cleros* again, or inheritance. Luke loves a good play on words.[6] The random lot becomes the mantle of inheritance. The chance becomes the choice of God in their midst. God teaches them how to trust God's providence.

Just as God called them, so God calls you. God calls and assembles people around you wherever you go and wherever God leads you, from this place forward, to be that band of brothers and sisters. When you are all alone, begin to reach out to others, pray psalms, and live together in community.

You've Been Given Another "Chance"

So let's review. You have been given a *cleros*—a chance or an inheritance. Now you need to make the choice. God does not have to dictate every decision in order for God to be involved in your lives, and every decision does not have to be perfect in order to stay in God's plan. Even one of Jesus' disciples "bought the farm." What God needs from you is a willingness to wait in the chaos, to renew your promises to the Christ who promised to be faithful to you, and to use psalms to see God's hand in the seemingly random moments of life. Will you crown Jesus as your Lord and stand on the promises that he is with you in this community, that he is calling new people to be in community with you wherever you go? Trust today and continue to trust, through the chaos, in the one who you have crowned Lord of all. Choose Christ in the midst of the inheritance. Psalms gives you a guidebook to hear Christ's voice with the community around you.

If God works in the chaos, then how does God work? God works so that when chaos comes, we wait for God to give us instructions. We return to Psalms and look back on where Christ is speaking. We huddle with the people who share this faith in Christ. And we turn again to the one in our midst, trusting God to give us discernment along the Way.

Sometimes the person you need has been with you all along. Gordon MacDonald tells the story of his experiences at Stony Brook High School.

On graduation weekend, his track team won the state championship. Since Stony Brook was a boarding school, the students were required to be back in the dorm by 11:00 p.m. or be disqualified from graduation. Coach Marvin Goldberg dismissed the team with specific instructions not to call him if they were going to be late. They left and met up with their girl-friends. No one got drunk or broke the law, but they did miss their train back to the station. A father was late picking up his daughter, and the boys did not want to leave the girls stranded. They waited with the girls and missed a train that would allow them to be back on time. They had broken the rules, but they were also showing good judgment. They realized the only person they could call to vouch for them was Coach Goldberg.

The Coach and his wife picked up the boys, delivered them to the dorms, and advocated for them to the principal. The boys graduated as planned. The Coach then told them, "From now on, you can call me Marvin."[7] Their experience changed the community, and it changed their relationship with their coach, too. In the chaos of Judas's loss, Peter and the early believers found their voice. God gave them another chance and provided community along the way. God will provide your band of brothers and sisters as you make the choice to crown God the Lord of all.

NOTES

1. Luke enjoys a good "play on words." Here he plays with the word *cleros* to indicate how close Judas was to enjoying the same benefits and blessings that Peter had. His life and Judas's are contrasted. Judas is left holding a field that becomes his cemetery. Matthias takes Judas's share in discipleship.

2. Robert Hendrickson, *The Facts on File: Encyclopedia of Word and Phrase Origins*, 3rd ed. (New York: Checkmark Books, 2004), 97.

3. Dietrich Bonhoeffer, *Life Together*, Gift ed. (New York: HarperSan-Francisco, 1993), 41.

4. Gordon MacDonald, *A Resilient Life: You Can Move Ahead No Matter What* (Nashville: Thomas Nelson, 2004), 198.

5. Bonhoeffer, *Life Together*, 43–44.

6. Mikeal C. Parsons, *Acts* (Paideia Commentaries on the New Testament) Grand Rapids: Baker Academic, 2008), 34.

7. MacDonald, *A Resilient Life*, 201.

3

Understanding Your Language

Acts 2:1–13

A sermon for Pentecost Sunday

The calendar is filled with important national celebrations.

The last Monday of May is Memorial Day. July 4 is Independence Day. November 11 is Veteran's Day. December 7 is Pearl Harbor. June 6 is D-Day.

Does anyone remember September 17? History teachers know that it is Constitution Day. We are free from Great Britain because of the publication of the Declaration of Independence on July 4 and the war that followed. We are a sovereign country of United States because of the charter document signed on September 17, Constitution Day.

For the church, Easter is Independence Day, a celebration of the freedom from sin and law because of Jesus Christ's death and resurrection. Pentecost is Constitution Day—the birth of the church and its charter by the Spirit. It happens with some remarkable signs attached, a power from on high.

How does this happen? According to the text, Jewish people are in Jerusalem from across the Mediterranean world. Many had moved there for various reasons and others were visiting. These were all Jewish, God-fearing people who believed in one God. The roll call of nations in Acts 2 sounds very much like Genesis 10, a list of nations from the surrounding area: Parthians, Medes, dwellers of Mesopotamia, and more. They tried to build a tower to heaven. It turned into a high-rise of hubris because everyone focused on their legacy. They tried to create a utopia:

literally "no-place."[1] God confused their common language, and the place was called Babel (Genesis 11).

Now, centuries later, the Jewish people in Jerusalem celebrate a different festival: the constitution of the Israelites at Sinai. God gave the law to Moses in Exodus, and Pentecost was the harvest festival scheduled fifty days after Passover.

Because of Jesus' resurrection, God makes a new covenant with a new Israel, the church. The Spirit appears to sign and seal the covenant. Inside an upstairs room where disciples wait and pray, something happens that changes them into a community. The Spirit shows. As Charles Talbert suggests, three things happen: audition (wind), vision (fire), and action (speaking and understanding).[2]

They hear the sound like a mighty rushing wind; they see a vision of fire. These Galilean disciples—whose accent was notoriously difficult to understand—speak in a dialect they have not used before. The Spirit empowers them to speak. The most remarkable part of this event, and the focus in Acts 2, is not the audition, vision, or commotion, but the power of the people to understand what the disciples are saying. Acts 2 repeats their understanding three times, in verses 8, 11, and 33.

Pentecost celebrates the birth of a community and the experience of deciphering the new language of community. By comparison, the people experience together what it is like to meet a new baby. At first babies are notoriously difficult to understand. Parents need time to decipher the hungry cry from the tired wail. When a child goes from crying to babbling to speaking, adults are able to discern a bit of what the child is saying. As they do, the adult and the child further bond and develop their relationship.

Easter is the holiday of individual salvation and the personal decision for Christ. Pentecost is the celebration of the community of Christ. The community is born. We do not retreat silently into our private worlds to come up with a few meaningful things to say, nor do we simply read a Scripture and remember Pentecost as something that happened long ago. Instead, the Lord repeatedly reunites, rebinds, and recommits us to each other as a church. Pentecost creates a living covenant community, uniquely united, bound, and committed for this moment in time and all this moment requires. The experience empowers the community to come together in an upstairs room and understand what the Lord says to them and to each other. Wherever two or three are gathered there shall be lots of opinions, but in Pentecost something happens to us and in us that says "Now we understand what we are to do."

If you travel to a foreign country, you try to learn some of the host country's language in order to speak and understand the natives. I had that experience on a mission trip to Germany with two years of German under my belt. We arrived at a small church without an interpreter, and I was called upon to translate. With my two years of conversational German, I knew very little about speaking or interpreting for others. Pentecost reveals a Spirit that interprets for us and empowers people to understand each other because of faith in Jesus Christ. On a recent trip to Israel, I experienced something closer to Pentecost. Next to the traditional site of the pool of Bethesda is a church built by the European Crusaders. Coincidentally, it is also one of the first stops on the Via Dolorosa, the way to Golgotha. Pilgrims often stop in the church because it is a good place to sing. Even tone-deaf people sound good in this chapel. When we entered, a Korean group was singing the hymn "God Is So Good" in Korean. We didn't understand the language, but we recognized the tune. Like good pilgrims, we hoisted our iPhones to capture the moment and sang along in our heart language. With tears flowing, we understood what these other believers were singing and saying.

Pentecost, however, is not a feel good, cozy, warm-and-fuzzy prayer meeting in a historic chapel for a private, though meaningful, moment. It is a noisy shakeup of our world that changes our lives. It sends us down the way of the cross to be changed into the kind of community Jesus wants to create.

Peter picks up on this theme in his sermon. He explains that the shake-up is a sign of the day of the Lord and a fulfillment of a prophecy from Joel. Now sons and daughters will prophesy and preach. Old men will dream dreams; young men will see visions. And everyone who calls on the name of the Lord will be saved.

The people interrupt, asking him what to do. Peter explains not only how to be saved but who they are being saved from:

> Repent and be baptized, every one of you, in the name of Jesus Christ
> for the forgiveness of your sins. And you will receive the gift of the Holy
> Spirit. The promise is for you and your children and for all who are far
> off—for all whom the Lord our God will call. With many other words
> he warned them; and he pleaded with them, "Save yourselves *from this*
> *corrupt generation.*" (2:38-40, emphasis mine)

We are being saved from a corrupt generation and born into a new family called the church. The Spirit is the power from on high to do this. It is the only power that you need, and you have already been qualified to do what you are doing. Understanding is a sign of salvation. Confused people still need to be converted. Listeners who understand the disciples are demonstrating evidence of salvation. It's further confirmation that the Lord intervenes.

As Peter declares to the crowd, the sign and signal that we understand what another person says comes through the Holy Spirit. Think how significant this could be for congregations with multiple generations. Some of us prefer to talk via text message while others would prefer to use the burnt orange rotary phone they had in high school. But when we come together through the power of the Spirit, we are able to sit and pray and listen and finally understand.

God has saved you from the other generation so that you can work together with this new community that the Spirit has given birth to: the church. This is not the last time the Spirit comes; it happens again in Acts 4, 8, 10, and 19. Nor is this the only sign of the Spirit. The gift of speaking in tongues is one sign, but it is actually a minor gift; sometimes the sign of the Spirit is prophecy, unity, or other gifts. No matter when the Spirit comes, one thing is constant: people actually begin to understand the gospel in their own language.

So what do we need to do? We need to sit and pray and seek to understand one another again. And we need God's help through the Spirit to do it. Just try to read some of the text messages from your teenager. You need a lexicon to keep up. Start talking in your grandparents' favorite phrases and even you probably won't know what you're saying. What will it take? The power of the Spirit teaches us how to understand another's language, not to try to figure out how to speak their language.

While working on my PhD at Baylor, I encountered a professor whom I thought singled me out. It took me three years to figure how he wanted me to think and write. I realized much later that this was all part of the process of education. At my dissertation defense, he was the first to arrive. Intimidated, I tried to strike up a conversation to find common ground. I knew he was active in his church and asked him how things were going. He replied, "They're going so well, we need a prayer ministry. I think you know what I mean." I finally understood what he was saying. And I did survive my dissertation defense and later reconciled with the professor.

So Happy Birthday, church. Today is your Constitution Day as a community. You have been born again, and there is a good chance we will finally understand.

NOTES

1. Eugene H. Peterson, *Christ Plays in Ten Thousand Places* (Grand Rapids: Eerdmans, 2005), 73.

2. Charles H. Talbert, *Reading Acts: A Literary and Theological Commentary on the Acts of the Apostles*, Reading the New Testament (Macon GA: Smyth & Helwys, 2005), 40.

4

King, Lord, and Christ

Acts 2:14-40

When I preach about Pentecost, I usually stop with the first half: the gathering in the upper room, the wind, the fire.

Admittedly, the story is much more exciting than Peter's sermon about the story. However, his sermon is just as important—and I would say compelling—for those who first heard the message as it is for us. Like a fireside experience after church camp, Pentecost is the church camp meeting story. But a song and a message shared around the campfire are both in Peter's sermon. He tells us to remember David, and that makes all the difference.

Remembering David

The tomb of David and the upper room are located on the same traditional site called the "Mount of Zion." Whether or not the two sites were historically connected, theologically Peter's sermon in Acts 2 connects them the way the visual sites are connected for tourists today. Both are memorial sites.

Pilgrims visit the traditional site of the upper room near the site of David's tomb on Mt. Zion. Even if David's burial and Pentecost do not occur in the same square block, the site makes the events easy to compare. In the disciples' minds, David and Pentecost are not far away.

King David is a prominent figure for Jesus' first followers. As is clear in the Gospels of Matthew and Luke and then into the Psalms, the Israelites saw this shepherd boy as the height of Judaism. In fact, even Jewish people today gather at the traditional site of this tomb to pray. Tradition said that the Messiah would come out of this line. He would be a king much like David. When the Messiah came, so said some rabbis, the world would come to an end and the Israelite nation would be in charge of the world. Everyone following Judaism would be placed under the Messiah's feet.

How does Peter convince a group of people that the world has changed? This transformation has not happened through a political dynasty or a patriotic rally. A new economic powerhouse will not begin, nor will a public works project. Instead, a group of people will center their lives on a Savior. To persuade them to follow Jesus, Peter explains that David has come. To do that, Peter changes their minds with music.

Songs for a Risen King

Peter takes a page from the old rabbinic book of Psalms and says, "Look with me at two very important psalms that are traditionally associated with David—Psalm 16 and Psalm 110." Think of these two psalms as the "Amazing Grace," and "Lord, I Lift Your Name on High" of the Hebrew hymnbook. Both of these songs answer the questions that Peter addresses in his message: If Jesus was born to an earthly mother, how can Jesus be God's son? How can the son of God also be a human? How can a human come from David's line?

Peter says that David saw it all along. Using a rhetorical technique called a *synkrisis*, Peter asks them to compare David and Jesus, drawing a verbal T-chart for the people to see. The chart looks like this:

David	Jesus
King	King
Jew	Jew
Judah	Judah
Political	Universal
Dead	Alive
Anticipated/Saw	Fulfillment

Peter reinterprets two psalms, commonly understood by his fellow Jews as conversations between the Lord God and the lord king David, as conversations between the Lord God and the Lord King Jesus. In much the same way that Psalm 22 foresees Jesus addressing God on the cross ("My God, my God," Psalm 22:1; Matthew 27:46), God speaks to God again in Psalms 16 and 110.

Peter says, "You will not abandon my soul to Hades" (Psalm 16:10; Acts 2:27), interpreting the verses as Jesus speaking to God, confident that God will provide for Jesus. This statement also addresses two challenges posed to the Way: could David ever be resurrected, and how could Jesus be the new Solomon? By his reinterpretations, Peter says that David himself anticipated a new king who would not abandon the Davidic line. David's line would continue and would not be abandoned to Hades. Jesus' resurrection restarts the Davidic line.

Second, Peter addresses Jesus' status as a Son of David by reinterpreting Psalm 110:1, "The Lord said to my Lord" (Matthew 22:44; Acts 2:34-35). Thus Jesus is now the new Son of David, addressing God directly. Through Jesus' resurrection, he is Lord. Peter tells the people listening that they have put their faith and hope in the wrong memory, the wrong king. They were hoping for David's line to begin through a new Solomon. But through Jesus' resurrection and the coming of the Spirit, Jesus inaugurated a new reign. Peter sees that someone greater has come, and now is the chance for the people to respond.1

An Unfolding Christian Testimony

Psalms 16 and 110 form part of the Old Testament *testimonia*. This is the repository of Scripture that the New Testament writers and speakers remembered, chanted, and passed onto their congregations. Using the Old Testament passages, they anticipated the future and planned for a better hope through Jesus.

Most Christians I know mistakenly think the testimony they have to share begins with the word "I" or includes the statement, "This is what God has done for *my* life." The apostles, however, realize their testimony is a story of God's intervention through Jesus. They do not talk about the difference Jesus made in their lives alone. They talk about Jesus' fulfillment of God's promise to the world.

In order to try to describe how Jesus makes such a difference, they go back to the Old Testament and see a great unfolding of God's promise. Like fabric being unfolded, the Old Testament Psalms are like one part of a very large tapestry God is revealing. Jesus fulfills dreams and expectations because he had always been a part of the plan.2 The testimony from Psalms shows how Jesus fulfills David's expectations.

Seeing Our Past as Preparation for Jesus' Reign

When we hear the Pentecost message, what is happening to us? Do our lives end with the comparison between David and Jesus? Or do we see our lives as a part of God's unfolding plan? The temptation is to see God's work end with David and Jesus, or to hide Jesus by tucking him away in our hearts. Peter's sermon calls for us to consider how everything in our lives that happened *prior* to meeting Jesus can be a part of God's preparation for us *to* meet Jesus.

Certainly not everything in your past is preparation, but so much of it is. Peter declares, "What we see as simply our past, God sees as a way to bring about the good news of the Spirit in our lives."

Preparing You for Jesus' Reign	Jesus as King, Lord, Christ
Parents	Jesus as New Family
Job	Jesus as New Calling
Friends	Jesus as Friends
Dreams	Jesus' Vision for the World
Sin	Jesus' Forgiveness
Guilt	Jesus' Freedom

See the list on the left side of the chart as God's way of preparing us for Jesus to reign over us. There is someone in the past who forms the fabric of your life. We thank God for the person who prepared you for the King's reign. Now we leave those loyalties behind and turn to Jesus. Pentecost does not just rekindle and spark a flame or blow a wind through our lives. Pentecost converts our loyalty to Jesus alone.

Christ's work cannot even compare to the events of our past. We can regret what happened. (Certainly the disciples had plenty of denials and a betrayal to regret.) We can desire more, say that we wish our lives had changed, or say that so much of our past is a way to look ahead and make sense of today. Jesus is ready to change who we are, what we are about, and what we are going to do. Now we are ready to respond, just as Peter's audience did.

What Shall We Do?

When Peter finishes revising his audience's memories of the past, the people say, "What shall we do?" Peter testifies not just of his own experience but also recounts the experience of the people in the Old Testament. They are linked to King David and King Jesus in order to rekindle, reignite, and set ablaze what God is doing in their hearts and world. The fire of the Holy Spirit forms and shapes the community. It changes how they remember the past so you can live as a testimony to them. You change what you remember. All of that anticipates the Jesus moment in your life.

The question for all of us is the question Peter's listeners asked, "What shall we do?" I faced a similar question in the Garden of Gethsemane a few years ago. I was talking with my favorite Israeli guide, a secular Israeli with a Jewish background. We were having a wonderful conversation comparing Christianity to Judaism and he asked me several questions about Jesus and the differences between our religions. Then he pressed further, "God's Son can't be both a human and God. If Jesus is God, how can there be a Judas?" I did not have the rhetorical skills of Peter, but I did respond with something like this: "Only the God of the universe could have enough power to allow a Judas to betray his own divine and human Son." Our guide asked, as so many others have done, "What shall we do about this Messiah?" Jesus' life and the Spirit's work demand decisions.

The conversations and questions are still there. Your past prepares you for a decision today to make Jesus your King and Lord. The Pentecost story never ends.

NOTES

1. This comparison technique occurs also in Stephen's speech. He compares Moses and Abraham. Paul does the same in Galatians, comparing life before and after Jesus.

2. I'm grateful to Dr. William Bellinger for this insight.

5

The Common Way

Acts 2:41–3:10

"We the people of the United States, in Order to form a more perfect Union…"

You probably recognize these words from the preamble to the Constitution, even if they bring up bad memories of civics class or social studies. But, as we hopefully learned in those classes, this charter document tells us what it means to be an American. No matter where you live across the United States, no matter what town you are in, our Constitution outlines a way of life that only applies to us. This document explains what sets this country apart from other countries and what sets you apart from citizens of other countries. When you are a citizen here, this is who you are. This is what you're about.

Pentecost is the church's Constitution Day. The book of Acts, though, is like the document itself. Acts describes the constitution of the church. When read, Acts requires more than silent reading or reflection: Acts must be performed by people. These are *acts*, not *thoughts*. Through the stories, habits, and actions, especially those recorded in chapters 1–12, the church lives out what its earliest members describe as the Way. The Greek word to describe their lifestyle is *koine* or *koinonia*. It's where we get our words "common," "company," "community," and "communication." Some translate this concept as "fellowship," as if it was an event on the calendar or an adjective to describe a room. Like the word "missions," often described as a periodic event, "fellowship" has been reduced to a punch bowl.

For the first Christians, fellowship equaled life. It was a common life marked by at least nine characteristics described in this passage. We are going to find them sprinkled throughout the book, but Acts 2:41–3:10 is like a revolving door. It sets the tone by reviewing where we have been, summarizing what we have seen, and previewing what is to come. At every stage of the book, you find people with signs and wonders in common.

Notice that the passage begins with baptism and ends with more conversion. In fact, baptism frames the story. What do you do with 3,000 converts? Baptize them into the fellowship. Then they leave, multiplying and seeking out more converts. In between, something powerful happens.[1]

In between these bookending conversions, a common life begins, and at its core is hospitality.

Conversions
    Common Life
        Signs and Wonders
    Common Life
Conversions

Think of it like a big, outward-focused potluck meal. Resurrection power draws people in. Everyone brings something to the table. People gather, break bread, and share what they have. A common way of living emerges that equips us to reach the unreached, uninvolved, and unchurched around us. This gathering is more than a Wednesday night supper or an after-funeral fellowship. This happens more often than simply Sunday mornings and Wednesday nights. This Way is life. The church grows like yeast in bread—organically. It grows out of the yeast of Judaism and enters into the living bread of Jesus' life in resurrection.

There are four characteristics in this passage that make the common life of followers of the Way unique:

Praying together,

Eating together,

Fellowship and sharing possessions,

Listening and responding to the teaching of the apostles.

On the surface, these elements might sound like a Christian version of a supper club. After all, for most people today, that is where community starts and stops. We get together, swap a few meals, and drop each other a casserole or two at the door when a loved one dies. We might join a support group during a time of grief or even read a Bible study written by a favorite author. We might even commit to this group for a couple of years because we will get information from it. When we leave, do we ever really know the people we were with?

Sociologist Robert Wuthnow studied support groups and small groups and realized that, in our loneliness and our isolation from one another, these small groups and information sessions can never really replace what the church and family are really supposed to be: the fabric, the community of life.

This problem goes back to Genesis 2. Somewhere in our lives, there has been a tearing. We know we were not made to be alone, and yet the fabric of family, or of our entire life, has been torn apart.

Here is the thing about Americans right now. We just do not want to be together the way we used to. We don't even like each other the way we used to. Sociologist Robert Putnam and many more have diagnosed the decline of civic engagement. Parents and children are thirty percent less likely today to take a family vacation. Forty percent of parents say they do not have free time to spend with their kids, mainly because of work. We entertain friends in homes about forty-five percent less than we did in the 1970s.

Why is that? Are we busy or selfish or all of the above? Or are we just lonely individuals who are looking to help ourselves, and what we really need is something only the church can provide? The church can become an outward-focused group that intentionally reaches out to people from all phases of life: the poor, the oppressed, the marginalized, the least, the last, and the lost. They find what they have in common and take this table on the Way with them. They start sharing their meals and developing what Bonhoeffer called a "life together."

Then, they report to each other the "signs and wonders" they have witnessed. For instance, look at the man in Acts 3:1-10 begging at the temple on Solomon's porch next to Peter and John. When Jewish people gave their temple sacrifice, they washed, climbed the steps, offered the animal, and then left the square and gave their alms to the poor. What they had missed all along, of course, is that their money was supposed to connect them, build relationships with those who, for physical or financial reasons, had been left out by their supposed community.

I had not quite understood this passage until I visited Jerusalem and saw where the poor waited for alms. They sat at the exit to the main temple courts so that the pilgrims would pass by after offering a sacrifice.

Peter and John had decided to pool their possessions with the people of the Way. Let the group handle the money. When these two apostles come out of the courts, a lame man had been waiting for forty years, carried along by this system. In those decades, an entire generation had been carried along by their religion, but they had never been community to him. He has been "carried" and left on the steps.

Peter and John have been carried along too . . . by the resurrection. When they spot the lame man, they look at him as a real person. They gaze at him; he gazes at them. "I don't have much money," Peter tells him. "It's pooled with these other people down the road. But what I do have to offer you is a whole new Way of living."

What this man needed and what these Christians had was some people in common. They were a part of a religious system with people from all phases of life, except his. The disabled were left out. Through this healing, he is now a part of the Way, a group of people who were outward-focused. They realized that, in order to be the people of the Common Way, they needed all God's people from all phases of life. The Way was the first inclusive community within Judaism, as they initially considered themselves to be. This was before they reached the Gentiles and had an identity crisis, by the way. Still, they were reaching out, as the prophets and Jesus did, to the disabled and ignored. Peter grabs the man by the hand, raises him up, and the man leaps as if he's stepped right out of Isaiah 35. Of course, this sign and wonder is reported to the people, as if to say, "Now take a look at this guy."

The resurrection takes a collection of individuals and turns us into a community. Instead of being carried along by our faith, we get devoted to our community, carrying out the disciplines of what it means to be on this Common Way.

How do we do that? By turning outward to the people who are being carried along by religion and carried along by others and saying, "Now we need to find something in common with them." Likewise, the early believers found people who were in their same phase of life, who needed Jesus, and they treated them like individuals. We share that back.

The Internationals ministry at First Baptist Church of Tallahassee, Florida, hosts an annual spring picnic. One year, Marty and Janice Smith, now retired, hosted a virtual United Nations potluck with duck, rice, mystery meats, and casseroles. Everyone brought their favorite foods from their home countries and invited their friends. There were Coptic Christians, Hindus, Buddhists, Muslims, and Christians. What they have in common is that they all need to learn English. What they shared together around the potluck are the signs and wonders of God's work around them.

Now, people bring bread and pimento cheese sandwiches on Tuesday and Thursday nights, and our group chows down during English classes. Some of them meet the Lord; others meet the Lord after they have left. All of them are on the way to joining the Way because of this ministry.

So where do we begin? We need to be devoted, persistent, doggedly determined to work on the four characteristics—praying together, eating together, fellowship and sharing possessions, and listening and responding to the teaching of the apostles—with people who are in all phases of life, especially yours. Start with the ignored in your midst. Many Christians struggle with this because, quite frankly, you actually can go it alone. You come to Christ through your individual response, and many people just want to keep it that way. It is hard to trust family; it is hard to trust friends. You can just be carried, lonely and alone, by what everyone else is doing. The staff can show up at the hospital, the teacher can teach the lesson, or the Christian Life Center can be open. But what if you didn't have to? What if there was a group of people who said, "You really need Jesus and I do too; let's do this together." That is the kind of community that really works.

"Look at me," the Lord says. "What if you could just be right here in community with us?" You have to do that together with someone else and with someone who needs what you have.

Amanda Shi participated in this potluck when she lived in Tallahassee. She met Jesus through the Internationals program but was not baptized until she moved to California. Her brief time in the First Baptist Tallahassee fellowship planted a seed for a lifetime of believing.

You are going to be in awe and amazed at what God does because of the Common Way. When you think you have got it figured out and you are sharing what's going on, God is going to show up in your life through a proverbial lame man, someone who you never saw coming. That will be the sign; yes Lord, I am finally on the Common Way.

What will you find as you share and eat with people whom you want to intentionally share life with? God will be doing things in them. You will find out what those things are and you'll report it back, just as Peter and John did. The process begins when we are doing the one thing that we share in common, communicating the life-giving resurrection power of the Lord Jesus Christ.

NOTE

1. This chiastic, or ring, structure is suggested by Parsons and Talbert. Mikeal C. Parsons, *Acts,* Paideia Commentaries on the New Testament (Grand Rapids: Baker Academic, 2008), 48. Charles H. Talbert, *Reading Acts: A Literary and Theological Commentary on the Acts of the Apostles,* Reading the New Testament (Macon GA: Smyth & Helwys, 2005), 50.

6

Faith in the Promise

Acts 3:11–26

Three years is barely enough time to educate a middle schooler, let alone Jesus' disciples. He left some unfinished business for them to complete. Their work began with someone the disciples and Jesus likely saw their entire lives.

Gazing at a Forty-Year-Old Lame Man

According to Acts 4, he is forty years old. That is long enough for the Israelites to wander in the wilderness and miss the promised land. It is long enough for Jesus to have seen him every time he went to the temple steps and he is old enough for disciples of a similar age to have seen him. There he is, next to Solomon's Portico. Jesus teaches there in John 10:22-39 but does not heal him. He leaves this man for the disciples to attend to later on. I imagine that they had seen this man in this spot their entire lives, every time they went to the temple. But now, because they trust in Jesus, they have something much greater than alms to offer him.

As the man extends his beggar's cup, Peter says, "Look at us!" We don't get to hear the man's voice at any time in chapters three or four, but we do see the results. Peter says that this time he will not give the man money. He will share something better than anything the man has ever received. The disciple raises him up, or as the text literally says, the man's "ankles became straight" again. The man is so excited that he starts leaping around. His literal knee-jerk reaction is so astonishing that he draws a crowd. People gather around staring at each other, looking at Peter, and probably saying to each other, "This is not what usually happens in Bible study." By the time the once-lame man has finished his "ten Lords a leaping" routine, he suddenly worries that something could happen to him. He holds onto

Peter's garment. In order to defuse a group of agitators, Peter explains to them what has happened. This speech is Peter's second sermon.

Miracles have many purposes in the Bible. Some are designed to teach, others to break in and show what is going to happen in heaven. In fact, Isaiah 35 says something like this would happen when the Messiah came. Isaiah 35 promises that, when the day of the Lord comes, "the lame will leap" (v. 6). The people are ready to worship the disciples, but Peter, pointing them to Christ, explains that this healing is a sign of the promise of things to come.

Reflecting on a Spiritually Lame Community

Solomon's Portico, where this healing and sermon occur, is the very spot where Jesus taught in John 10:22-39, and Peter uses this formerly disabled man as a mirror. This guy is a reflection of generations of people who have been left on the steps of religion around their temple. We are just like him. We are not physically disabled, but we are spiritually ignorant. We think we have all the facts and know how things are always going to be, but we really know very little about Jesus. We are pursuing religion in all the wrong places, and this guy who has been sitting at the gates of Solomon's Portico for decades knows more than we do. But for him and for us, one name changes everything: Jesus.

The sign of the lame man. What happens to this guy in Jesus' name is the same thing that can happen to you and to us. In this person, Peter sees a community of marginalized people. The lame man is a sign of who they were. He lacks a physical ability; the people lack spiritual ability.[1] For forty years they had been shut out by religion, by the church. They are uninvolved and unchurched, and many of them are just unsaved. But the reality is there is a new urgency here. Jesus has come and is returning, and he wants them to be a part of the promise of God's restoration in their lives. And a formerly disabled man leaping around outside a temple gate is just one sign of the promise.

"What we need though," says Peter, "is not more information. We need a transformation that can only happen through faith in a promise, the promise that this same Jesus who died and was resurrected, whose power healed this man, will come again to bring restoration.

"The same God that called Abraham in Genesis has now sent Jesus into the world. Jesus is the new Isaac, an only son dedicated as a sacrifice, one who has come back to life as the Prince of life. Even though you rejected him, he's now reigning in heaven. You had no idea what you were doing. Living in sin clouds your mind and messes with your judgment. If you repent and return, times of refreshing may come, and God will wipe away your sins; he will send Jesus."

Now this is an interesting point. Peter not only anticipates that God is going to send Jesus to your heart and to your life, but Peter also anticipates what is going to happen next in verse 21; God is going to send Jesus for a period of restoration. The prophets have spoken about such a promise.

The promise of Jesus' return. Now God has intervened and sent Jesus, who died on the cross for the sins of Israelites, Romans, and everyone else. Christ has come back to life. He has been raised from the dead. We live in a time when the resurrection has happened, but the new age has not yet begun. When Christ ascends, he leaves behind a new Israel called the Way to represent his mission to the world. As heralds and messengers, they show and demonstrate that Jesus' salvation is the only hope we have. We await his promise to restore all things.

Instead of destroying the world by fire, he wants to redeem and restore it. But the work is incomplete. There is still work to be done. And one day Jesus is going to complete that work himself. But, in order to do that, he wants to issue an invitation to anyone who wants to come and join the family.

When we think about eternity, usually we are thinking about two things: how are we going to get to heaven, and what is the proof that heaven exists. Most bestsellers focus on the place or the journey in order to give *us* greater security and assurance. The only proof of heaven we need, however, is Jesus' presence.

Jesus says in John 14, "I am going to prepare a place for you." This means he will prepare the place and location. Our job is to trust that he, like a groom, will return and "receive us unto himself" (v. 13).

What animates the disciples in Acts is the promise that Jesus will return. As he ascended, the angel gave the disciples a promise: "This same Jesus will return in the same manner you have seen him go into heaven" (Acts 1:11).

The healing of the lame man is the first sign that Jesus keeps his promises. He said the disciples would do signs and wonders, so here is some evidence. "You think this is good? Just wait until Jesus returns. This is what is going to happen to every person who needs healing, and every marginalized, ignored, and mistreated person. In the meantime, share this promise with those you know. New life flows again around this temple, through a relationship with Christ, and this man is evidence of it. A whole new generation of people—the church—can be God's agents of reconciliation and restoration to people. And this man is one of them! He is the sign of the Messiah's coming . . . and coming again."

Peter tells the crowd that, just a few weeks ago, they were the ones who crucified their one chance to have new life again. Despite their destruction of the only righteous man to ever live, Jesus came back to life, and his resurrection offers them a chance to change, to repent. Or, in this man's case, to be healed of the very thing that has defined their existence. They can allow the river of God's life to flow again.

Reaching the Spiritually Ignorant around Us

Here is our problem. Instead of reaching across to the people we have isolated, socially or individually, we are usually pondering the pearly gates. We are surrounded by people who are dried-up, empty, and left on the steps of religion, people who desperately need a time of refreshing. Even the Jewish people in Jesus' day believed in an afterlife. Most religions do, and so do we. In fact, heaven is a wonderful destination. But Jesus and his disciples' focus was not so much on the place where we would go, but on Jesus' journey to us: "I will come again and will take you to myself, so that where I am, there you may be also" (John 14:3). That will be another gift from God, that Christ will come and get us, that he will come back here for you, that things are going to happen that you cannot explain, but no matter what, Jesus will be the one to come back and receive you unto himself.

When I served as pastor of First Baptist McGregor, Texas, we went every Wednesday morning for nursing home services. One of our helpers was David, a preacher and minister about my age with Down syndrome. David was under the care of his Baptist mother and his Lutheran father. He had business cards and he ministered with us. There is no doubt in my mind he was one of the best ministers we had. He could relate to the people there and they could relate to him much better than I could. One week, a woman showed up for the services who was elderly and disabled, and she had a lady, Laura, with her. David and his mom visited with her and struck up a friendship. Soon this woman named Laura started coming to church, and of course, a community of people in this small church began to surround them. Eventually, we asked Laura about her husband, Tommy.

Tommy said, "Preacher, I'll never come to church, but what I'd like to do is invite you and the church to come out to our house for barbecue sometime." I said that would be fine. He hosted us. Later in life, I discovered that Jesus had a term for this kind of person—a person of peace. Tommy had faith, just not faith in Jesus. Like people in Luke 10, Matthew 10, and Acts 11, they host the people who have the conversations about Jesus. Eventually, they believe in Jesus.

Here was this lost person hosting us in his home and showing hospitality. After a few times doing this, I said, "Tommy, why don't you ever come to church?" And he told me a story. Forty years ago, he attended a church of another denomination. It could have been any Christian denomination; the issue is endemic to all of them. When his son died, the minister left town to go to a meeting. The church never called, and Tommy felt abandoned. He promised that he would never darken the door of the church again. Of course, David's outreach and that visit were just the beginning of a process that Christ works through all of his disciples, even bumbling preachers.

The Spirit Reaches Us

When we reach across to the spiritually hindered, the Spirit does five things through us. I can remember this with an acronym: REACH.

Restores creation. The lame man and Tommy were created but isolated individuals. The disciples do the work of reconciliation to restore all things to the Creator.

Educates the ignorant. By reaching across to the isolated, we overcome our ignorance. Religious people can be just as ignorant as the uneducated Galilean fisherman. Those who win Bible Trivial Pursuit can be just as cloudy as those who have never been to middle school. Christians have all the training they need and certification through their baptism to share the gospel.

Advances the gospel. When we reach across to the unreached, the gospel advances. It is that simple. Acts 28:28 says that the gospel continued unhindered. That is the theme of Acts: not Paul, not Peter, not Lydia, but the unhindered gospel.

Calls for commitment. When we do reach out, there is a time of urgency. Now, not later. The promise is to respond now, before Jesus returns and it is too late. There are eternal consequences for procrastination. By responding now, we experience a time of refreshing promised to all who believe.

Heals our lives. Responding and reaching across heals our lives. The lame man was healed, and so are we.

The same thing that happened to this man on the steps of Solomon's Portico can happen to us because we still have some unfinished business. Jesus left a person for the disciples to reach. The disciples left others for the church to reach. Even pastors leave unfinished work for successors to complete, like Tommy. I did not see Tommy come to know the Lord as Savior. My successor did. About a year after that, Tommy was baptized. About two years later, he was diagnosed with stage 4 terminal cancer and died. But he passed away with faith in the promise of Christ.

Three years is not very long, but it is just long enough to reach across to someone you have seen your entire life. Today is the day of salvation.

NOTE

1. This is suggested by Mikeal C. Parsons in *Body and Character in Luke and Acts* (Grand Rapids: Baker Academic, 2006), 121–22.

7

At the Feet of Authority

Acts 4:1–5:16

After Peter and John healed the lame man and spoke to the crowd, you can imagine that the religious authorities were none too pleased with this community in and around their temple. So once Peter and John were released from prison through the power of God, they gathered and started praying. In Acts 4:31, they prayed for boldness. The whole place was shaken. What happened next was even more amazing: they submitted their possessions to someone else's authority.

You might think it was some random thing that a lame man now stands on his feet and leaps around like he is straight out of Isaiah 35. But this was a movement of people on the Way. They gathered to follow Christ with their feet. When they finally got back together to ask God for boldness, notice what happens.

It is mentioned three times in the text. It's a little phrase. Once would be enough. Twice would add emphasis, but according to the speech writers in Luke's day, if you wanted to drive home the point and leave a deep impression on the people and the opposition, you repeat it over and over again.[1] It happens in 4:35, 37; and 5:2. The little phrase is simply "at the feet."

Feet in Luke

This phrase is not the first time that Luke had thought a lot about feet. In Luke 7:38, a woman stands behind Jesus' feet, wets, wipes, kisses, and anoints them. In Luke 8:35, a formerly demon-possessed man sits at the feet of Jesus. In Luke 8:41, Jairus falls at Jesus' feet and begs him to come to his house. In Luke 10:39, Mary sits at Jesus' feet listening to his word.

Throughout Luke and now in Acts, the feet were the place of submission to authority. If you wanted to know who was in charge, you watched whose feet people went to. So in Acts, when it is time for the offering, the interesting catchphrase in Acts 4:23–5:11 is not how much people gave, or what they did with the money, but the fact that they were willing to be in community with others and that they trusted these others to know how to handle their possessions. You guessed it, see it in their feet.

At the Feet of the Apostles

This text is a comparison and contrast. On the one hand you have Joseph, who sails from Cyprus and becomes enamored with this movement of the Way. In fact, the resurrection so changes his life that he wants to be a part of the movement. He goes back home, sells some property, and brings the proceeds from the real estate transaction and turns it over to the apostles. He lays it at their feet.

On the other hand you have the husband-wife team of Ananias and Sapphira, who decide that they too want to be a part of this group. In fact, they apparently already are. But when it comes time to sell land, they keep a portion of the money for themselves and lay the rest at the apostles' feet. Eventually both die, Sapphira at Peter's feet.

When I have preached on this before, I wanted to get into the head of Barnabas. I wanted to describe the motives of Peter and Ananias and Sapphira. But in my estimation, the key here is not the apostles, Barnabas, or Ananias and Sapphira. It is the act of submission. It is the mentality of this community that someone knows better than I do what to do with the money. The same people who prayed for boldness are actually the same people who know what to do when we get together and start sharing our possessions.

Responding to Prayers for Boldness

What happens when you pray for boldness, the Holy Spirit's power is revealed, and people turn their lives around? People usually react in one of two ways. They either lay their resources at the apostles' feet, fully surrendering to the Lord, or they try to stay in charge and maintain control while pretending to go along with everyone else.

The phrase "at the feet" marks one of the characteristics of this charter for a Common Way: submitting possessions to someone else's authority.

This is not a blind loyalty to the apostles. Later in Acts, the Holy Spirit will direct them where they are to go. The point of submission is not directed toward the recipients. The gesture itself shows that the disciples are willing to come together in community, to lay their own things down, and to give someone else authority to decide what to do with them.

When we talk about a community sharing possessions, the first thing we wonder is what they are going to do with them. The problem is on the leaders, not us. Obviously the whole thing is fraught with danger and peril. We might think, as we would be prone to do in our world, about what they might do with this money. In a world of open records laws and clergy scandals, it always behooves us to keep close tabs on what *they* might do.

The real cause of corruption in the early church was not what the apostles did with the resources but who was given the resources. Would the people be willing to share and give everything, trusting in submission to the Lord?

The resurrection changes how we use our possessions. In order to share the gospel to the ends of the earth, we must trust others with what Christ has given us. This act of obedience and trust is another sign of the resurrection life.

We Need Authority Figures

Part of what we demonstrate to the larger world is the power of submission to authority. Usually we think about this only in marriage—we submit to the Lordship of Jesus Christ in our households. But submission is also something that we do in the church. We submit to the authority of someone else (or a group of someone else's) and allow that person (or group) to disperse, redistribute, and extend the mission with what we call our possessions.

One of the struggles in the modern world, especially since the mid-1990s when support groups and small groups became the primary way that people grew spiritually, is that we lost something that Robert Wuthnow and Randy Frazee diagnosed. We need someone in our lives to tell us that we are wrong.[2] This is something that parents and families do most every morning. They say, "You're going to wear that?" "You need to cut the grass this way and not that way."

In lots of little daily things, parents and family members give guidance in our lives. We think they're being annoying; they're just being a community.

One of the things that groups cannot provide for us is the sense that we are not in charge. Often times when we join a book club, we join it because we think they will want to hear what we have to say. When we get involved in a support group, we'll actually say that they will support us. As Robert Wuthnow found, none of these can actually do for you what real community can do and tell you. A real community will say, "You're not as smart as you think you are. You might actually be wrong. You might actually need someone to tell you what to do." We actually do not know what to do.

Randy Frazee notes that a study indicated 1 in 5 adolescents had seriously contemplated suicide and that 30% of teenagers had engaged in binge drinking. The report suggested that what was needed was not more medication but more communication. The people needed an authoritative community in their lives to provide guidance and care.

We actually need authority figures in our lives, and we need each other for correction, instruction, and submission.

I remember having one of those times with my wife Kelly when we were both busy and running around. And she said that we needed to talk. This was one morning, and I was kind of glancing at the paper and listening. And she said, "Put the paper down, and listen to me. Listen to *me*. You're not so smart after all. You listen to all these people all week long. It's time for you to listen to me."

We need people to be in charge of us. We need people who lovingly correct us. As Acts 4 and 5 suggest, the hardest conversation that we have is not with what happens to the possessions when they are given; it is the conversation that happens before the check gets written. Are we willing to allow someone else to decide what to do with this check, these resources, these possessions?

Doing so is a witness that our lives are not our own, and that we have been given gifts for a certain community so that this group of believers can extend God's provisions beyond the walls and into the community. We were wired for someone else to be in charge.

The real difference between Barnabas and Ananias and Sapphira is that one is willing to surrender control and the others want to remain in control. Ananias and Sapphira keep back a portion of what belongs to them. In the end, they don't trust with the apostles with it, and this act kills them.

Barnabas is willing to come and lay the money at the apostles' feet because these were the people extending the mission of the church in the world. Ironically, the apostles were probably not in charge of the church. The apostles were actually the ones "sent out" from the church to go extend the gospel to other places. Someone else was actually in charge. The great irony of the story is that the apostles leave. Someone else oversees it.

Every summer, many churches like mine send summer missionaries and teams across the world. A finance committee oversees the disbursement, but these missionaries go. Individually, we may have no idea how to accomplish this work. When we give, we trust the people who know how to take care of this place. We want the ministry to continue and the place to grow because we have missionaries here.

So the question is never about what the apostles or the overseers are going to do with it. We already know what they are going to do. They are sharing the message. The question is always: how much are we willing to trust someone else's authority?

Do we trust the God of the universe to say, "I want to depend on you so much that someone else is going to be extending this work and meeting needs around the world"? We will know who does simply by watching their feet.

NOTES

1. Mikeal C. Parsons, *Acts*, Paideia Commentaries on the New Testament (Grand Rapids: Baker Academic, 2008), 74.

2. Randy Frazee, *The Connecting Church 2.0* (Grand Rapids: Zondervan, 2013), Kindle edition.

8

Putting God's Plan in Place

Acts 5:17-42

Where do you feel right at home? Often it is not the place you sleep. Instead, your office colleagues or church friends feel more like family than those you are related to biologically. What if God had a plan for the places where you lived, worked, played, and worshiped? What if God saw those as a unified, holistic life, not as compartments of existence?

In the resurrection, people from temple, home, city, and work spheres came together, gave themselves to the place where God had put them, and formed a new community.

A Plan

This story begins following the death of Ananias and Sapphira. The apostles move to Solomon's Portico on the edge of the temple complex where Peter and John healed the man in chapter 3. Word spreads that even Peter's shadow can heal the sick. This success upsets the religious leadership, so they order Peter and John to stop teaching in the temple courts and place them in the religious jail. That night, they are miraculously released from the prison. When the authorities order them to testify, Peter and John announce that they must obey God and plan to keep doing what they are doing.

After a puzzling response from the leadership, Gamaliel suggests that there is a plan in place. Someone behind the scenes is lurking. Much like Pilate's announcement that Jesus indeed is the Son of God, now Gamaliel realizes there is a plan. He is not sure if it's God's plan. If it is, they will have to watch and see to find out. So they order these two apostles to be beaten and released.

But how do the apostles know if a plan is God's plan? How do we? Everyone needs a plan; you cannot just become a community on your own. We know we need people, we need to share our possessions, and we need a way to accomplish the plan. What is that plan, and how do we know if it's working?

In Jerusalem, twice weekly, they received a collection for the poor. Three people went house to house to take up an offering. The produce and money were redistributed and then given to those who needed it, like the widows and orphans. Another three would go house to house to take up an offering for complete strangers who had nothing to eat whatsoever. That was the routine of an average Jewish life. They did not have a strategy per se; it was simply their custom. The apostles realized that they had a plan; they needed a location to accomplish the plan.

Places

Every plan needs a place, and the apostles give themselves two: the temple and the house. Acts 5:42 says that they went to the temple and from house to house. Let's look at the contrast between the two.

Temple	House
Worship	Work
Purity	Hospitality
Separate	Family
Tradition	Spontaneity

What if you could combine the two and create a way of life? This would be a community where both could come together from temple and house, take the best of both worlds, and integrate them into a common life. What would that look like, what kind of plan would they need, and how would they ever get there?

Before we identify the method, we must admit that we struggle to keep our worlds separate. We get home late, we live for ourselves, and we struggle with the reality that everything is all one holistic piece. Just ask any mother today. You cannot separate responsibilities of home, work, and church. And in God's eyes, our lives are all one big piece.

The ancient world saw work and home as the same thing. The apostles built on this concept and brought work, worship, and worth all together. Faced with their own mortality and death, they changed their priorities. Their lives were threatened. They were beaten. Ironically, the first thing that they do when they fear for their lives is to take care of neglected widows murmuring against the Greeks and others.

I love this scene, because it describes what church is really like. These guys are really threatened. Instead of trying to draw more attention to the problem, they realize widows are not being fed. Their administration has broken down.

Much like today, we can have a great Easter Sunday worship and, by Monday, be suddenly thrown back into reality of the world. Their troubles are transfigured in one day. The apostles see this as an opportunity.

The late Kent Haruf called this concept the "precious ordinary." It is the rather spontaneous, frequent, everyday routine of the daily lives of work and home that become so important in our routine lives as Christians. These are the places where people need community now more than ever, in the precious ordinary of life. With the coworker whose husband dies, the neighbor whose daughter dies, and the child whose father dies, God calls us to share the resurrection and to minister. We take what we learn from the temple and go to a place—the homes and workplaces of our lives—and share the gospel through what we do. That was the plan. We carry it out because we have faced up to our own mortality. Through our baptism, we have been buried with Christ and raised to walk in newness of life. We are suddenly faced with the reality that our lives and even our families are not our own, so God calls us to the place where we live; nothing fancy, just ordinary routine. This is a place where they could be frequently available to each other.

Baptism confronts us with the reality that we have been buried with Christ and, one day, will meet him again. We are given to the place where God, who liberates us, has called us. What do we do there? I would like to suggest four things using the SAFE acronym.

A SAFE Plan in Your Place

Spontaneous traditions: Look around for spontaneous, fun ways to break into the routine at home, work, church, or school.

Available lives. Make time and room in your calendar for people to drop in. Be available to them and be fully present. Reduce your schedule to allow for flexibility.

Frequent contact. Check on a neighbor, a coworker, and a friend. The apostles went house to house checking on people. Develop an intentional system with your kids and family. Talk about where God is working in your life and where you are struggling with God.

Rick Howerton says, "What happens between Sundays affects what happens on Sunday." If life is happening between Sundays, then when we come back to Sunday we will be different. If we are living in community at work and home, then on Sunday, the community grows and develops on its own.

This is something that mothers know. In her book *All Joy and No Fun,* Jennifer Senior describes Sharon, who after adopting her grandchild learned that she was dying. Sharon was sixty-seven. She had adopted Cam when one of her daughters passed away from cervical cancer at the age of thirty-two. Cam was born at twenty-eight weeks and his mother only lived nine more months. If that was not hard enough, another of Sharon's children had taken his own life at age sixteen. Sharon lived alone on a fixed income. She was surrounded by friends and loved ones and a church family, but most people would still say she had no business raising a child. People would assume that she would be far happier, at her age and in her position, without a child. But in reality, Sharon felt extremely fulfilled.

Senior writes,

> The problem of adulthood, of course, is it just makes us brittle and ungenerous in judgments toward others. Little kids go a long way toward yanking grown-ups out of their silly preoccupations and cramped little mazes of self-interest—not just relieving their parents of their egos but helping them aspire to something better. [1]

Cam did that for Sharon, but now Sharon is dying. "You can't be a person of faith," she said, "and not have thought a lot about dying." For a few months, she tolerated the chemo well. She was well connected and never lacked for home-cooked meals. But she soon realized she could not care for her grandson any longer. She reorganized; she made plans to move. Another member of the family would take Cam. He will be part of a family with two parents and other young children.

Senior continues:

Parents generally do not grapple with the fact of their own mortality
from day to day. But if they are forced to, as Sharon was, something can
happen. The clarity of their role, rather than its complexity, comes into
view. Meeting obligations, arranging for the future, communicating
unconditional and eternal love, these become the primary tasks of a
parent who is dying. What such a parent does, if she has little kids, is
lead as normal a life as possible, only with more pancakes. Sharon said
she felt guilt and relief at the prospect of dying, guilt that she was
abandoning Cam and relief that he would have two parents to take care
of him…I'm trying to be present and spend a lot of time watching
Curious George, normal life, with more pancakes.[2]

Normal life, more pancakes. Why would we wait until the end? We already
know our lives are buried together with Christ by baptism. Let's rise to walk
in newness of life in the place God has put you. You are the plan he has put
into place.

NOTES

1. Jennifer Senior, *All Joy and No Fun: The Paradox of Modern Parenthood*
(New York: Ecco, 2015), Kindle edition.

2. Ibid.

9

Performance of the Gospel

Acts 6

Our first home had two kinds of grass: St. Augustine in the backyard and Bermuda in the front. The lawn was beautiful . . . when we bought the home. Having never been homeowners, and certainly not familiar with specific lawns, I felt a sense of accomplishment just mowing the grass regularly. Little did I know that the very act of cutting the lawn spread seeds from one kind of grass to another. By mowing, I was also sowing. The Augustine spread to the front yard. The Bermuda that scattered to the back never seemed to take root. Weeding would have taken as long as mowing. Eventually, I surrendered to the process and let the Augustine go wherever it wanted.

In Acts 6, something similar happens to the Way. Beginning with Acts 6:7 and continuing to the end of chapter 12, a theme brackets the Jerusalem church.[1] The theme can be understood by this phrase, which says, "The word of God continued to spread; the number of the disciples increased greatly in Jerusalem, and a great many of the priests became obedient to the faith" (Acts 6:7). Just as Jesus predicted in Luke 8, the word of God increased like seed sown from one place to another. As it did, the disciples multiplied.

Word of God in Acts

There are three kinds of "words" described in Acts. First, the word of God from the Old Testament Scriptures is used as the believers' base for discussions with fellow Jews. Second, the word of God is the "word made flesh" (John 1:14) in the resurrected Jesus. Third, the disciples perform Christ's words through the power of the Spirit. How is that possible? They take the Scriptures and interpret them.

That is not typically how we study the Bible. We read a verse devotionally, usually reflecting on the question, "What does this passage mean to *me*?" Group study centers on the historical background, questions, and dialogue. But most people generally want to know what they can take away from the passage and apply to their lives.

The Way studied the Bible like a book club without a book. The group dynamics were just as important as the content. Drawing from an active, engaged memory of the Old Testament, they dialogued, debated, and challenged each other. The people in the room were usually not believers in Jesus. The room felt more like the synagogue in Luke 4. Someone might read a passage, sit down, and wait for a response.

For example, in Acts 6, Stephen has one of these Bible debates in the synagogue of the Freedmen. This place is fascinating because the very people who will later become the central figures of Acts are from this area. Cyrenians, Alexandrians, and others of those from Cilicia and Asia argue with him. Ironically, Saul of Tarsus was from Cilicia.

Of course, the people do not agree with Stephen. That part is not unusual. He stands to speak, and the Spirit intervenes. As Jesus predicts in Luke 12:12, the Spirit gives words of wisdom to Stephen. Spirit, word, and wisdom are the three necessary components for this gift. Stephen does not talk about his life. He retells the stories of Joseph and Moses. Joseph is sold by his brothers into slavery in Egypt but relates words of wisdom in the Pharaoh's house. Moses is taught the wisdom of the Egyptians before he becomes the leader of the Israelites.

Stephen is a powerful example for anyone who engages the Scriptures. Stephen demonstrates how the Old Testament passages, the word made flesh in Jesus, and Jesus' words can scatter the word of God.

When we are engaged in this way with nonbelievers, the Spirit gives us the words of wisdom to say. Whoever is an opponent of the gospel cannot withstand what we have to say. Verse 10 says, "They could not withstand the wisdom and the Spirit with which he spoke."[2]

Performing the Word

Early Christians approach the Scriptures the way choir members study music or members of a theater troupe prepare Shakespeare. The music and the play come alive when they are performed. We can study the pages as long as we want but, until they are presented on stage, they are just notes and words on a page.

I remember my first piano recitals. People came who could not play the piano, and some could play much better. They were supportive of me and my attempts to make music.

The early church found that until they spoke, interpreted, and shared the gospel, the message was worthless. When they did, the Holy Spirit became present and offered them words of wisdom. All three worked together. Look at the diagram below to visualize the interplay among the three.

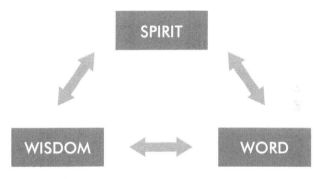

Spirit: the empowered and inspired gift that came at Pentecost

Word: the word of God from the Scriptures, revealed in Christ, spoken on their lips

Wisdom: what to do with the message they received, what they believed, why they believed it, and how to apply it in their context

The people these faithful believers began to affect were inspired by what Stephen did. His life and death affected others, especially Saul.

One of my friends and former church members started a group in his neighborhood for this very purpose. He wanted to invite some neighbors who were not attending church. They shared meals together for a while. When one of them went through a crisis, they said, "Why don't we start reading Scripture together and praying after we eat?" One thing led to another, and then they began to meet together in our home for prayer, conversation, and accountability. My friend said to me, "Do you know who the most faithful people are to this group? The people who are not church people. They say, 'We need this because we don't get it on Sundays.'"

That is precisely what happens in the early church. They come together in a bold initiative, and their word spreads like seed everywhere. What do we need to prepare for the Spirit, word, and wisdom that will be given? I would suggest to you that we follow the disciples' pattern.

Begin by serving people. Live on mission already. Do not try to be appointed a deacon or a leader; simply serve. Form friendships with non-believers. Have discussions with unreached people. By sowing this seed, you nurture the sprouts in your life. As you practice the stories, you are preparing for the recital.

When the audience looked at Stephen, his face was like the face of an angel. They saw in his life the kind of person that they wished they could become if they could just get out of the group they were in. His life reflected back to them what they needed to be.

If someone used your face as a mirror, what would they see? Would they see a person that they aspire to be or a person that sows seeds of discord, hate, violence, and fear? The word multiplies because of people like Stephen who serve, share, and prepare to distribute the word wherever it multiplies, even if they have to pay the ultimate price.

When you stand and testify, you will not need to rehearse what you are to say. The Spirit will be there to give the words to you. That's the wisdom you need.

So dust off the pages. Let's perform together. Watch the word multiply.

NOTES

1. Mikeal C. Parsons, *Acts*, Paideia Commentaries on the New Testament (Grand Rapids: Baker Academic, 2008), 12.

2. Something similar happens in Acts 4:31; 12:24; and 19:20.

10

The Pursuit of Joy

Acts 7:1–8:8

The thermos company YETI has revolutionized the idea of the thermos, travel mug, and cooler. Maintaining the thermos's internal temperature for an extraordinary length of time, YETI products keep hot drinks hot and cold drinks really cold.

People can often work like liquids. Over time a person's strong feelings tend to become more tepid. But like coffee poured into a good thermos, when people unite for a purpose, whatever is inside a person becomes even more noticeable. The unity of a group that shares the same concerns can make you violent, upset, mean spirited, and even destructive. Unity can also lead to salvation and joy. In the early church, we discover two side-by-side examples.

Acts uses a word that is located in only one other place in the New Testament—*homothumadon*. The word literally means "same thermal," as if we were united in the same pursuit. Scholars translate the word as "together," "with one accord," or "without exception." The interesting thing to me is that the word is used differently with believers than with opponents. And the two come together right here. To see how this works, compare the lists below.

Two Kinds of Unity

Believers
Praying (1:14)
Together in one place (2:1)
Attending the temple (2:46)
Lifting their voices to God (4:24)
Signs and wonders in Solomon's Portico (5:12)

Multitudes in Samaria give heed (8:6)
Appointing Barnabas and Paul (15:25)

Opponents
Stoning Stephen (7:57)
People of Tyre and Sidon to Herod (12:20)
Attack on Paul (18:12)
Ephesian attack on Gaius and Aristarchus (19:29)

United in vengeance. Notice how closely "united" and "vengeance" occur in chapters seven and eight. On the one hand, the opponents are united against Stephen. When they saw him, the Lord reflected in his face. Like the people's reaction to Jesus in Luke 4 and Luke 22, Stephen's opponents are upset by what they see and hear.

Stephen preaches a mighty sermon as a deacon. He draws a contrast between the generation of Moses and the generation of Abraham. He places the religious leaders in the category of Jewish people who killed the prophets. He compares the followers of the Way to the true followers of God. This is not the kind of sermon designed to win people over, but it does have a certain effect on the crowd. The sermon unites them, and they are enraged. They grit their teeth. Their passion and fire burns deeply. They stiffen their necks and unite in their desire to get rid of Stephen. They are critical of Stephen, stone him, and are stiff necked and stubborn.

This kind of unity causes vengeance, fear, and bodily changes. Today you can feel it when your blood pressure rises, when television or radio commentators scream, and even when sports fans get upset. Social media becomes the garbage dump for this kind of language and vitriol. As Gary Fenton says the rhetoric is like "verbal litter."

United in joy. Something changes, however, in Acts 8:6. The disciples scatter because of the Jewish people's vengeance, rage, and stoning of Stephen. The believers undergo their own diaspora—a scattering—and the first disciple to head north into foreign territory, and to fulfill Acts 1, is a deacon named Philip. He doesn't preach like Stephen. His opponents are different; they are Jewish Samaritans. They worship in other places. They are prone to rejection. The disciples wanted to call fire down on one of the Samaritan villages (Luke 9:54). Now a deacon is in their town.

These Samaritans already have a kind of faith healer and self-help magic man in their midst named Simon. He is a David Copperfield or David Blaine type. Simon symbolizes the instant results preached by

Joel Osteen, Creflo Dollar, and many so-called megachurches. Things always seem to work so well for these overnight sensations, and they continually point people toward more resources produced and published by the individuals who found and grow these massive churches. Whether through books, videos, or the Internet, these magic individuals exist for the purpose of perpetuating themselves. Like these pastors and individuals, Simon sees Jesus as a way to make life work better for him and to draw more attention to himself.

The Way doesn't come with easy fixes, quick answers, or overnight solutions. It directs people away from any one person (or brand) and toward Jesus. Philip offers them the signs that point to a Savior, to a common purpose beyond themselves, and a deep connection with others. The Samaritans share a pursuit of meaningful relationships that reach beyond ethnic and religious boundaries. Philip declares that Jesus is the King of kings and Lord of lords. Despite the success of Simon, the people were united and responded without exception (*homothumadon*), and the whole city is filled with joy.

Vengeance Versus Joy

Unity can result in either vengeance or joy. Both groups pursue change in their cities. In vengeance, one unites to preserve what they know from the past. In joy, one unites on a mission in a common pursuit of the kingdom of God. Arguably, the Pharisees and religious leaders wanted to keep Jerusalem clean. The Samaritans wanted their businesses to do the same. What made the difference? When confronted with the gospel, one led to joy and the other led to anger, resentment, and revenge. The difference lies in the direction of their pursuit.

The religious leaders preserved what they knew from their past. They filled their lives with anger, vengeance, and hate for someone who changed the status quo.

The Samaritans wanted to change a city. They responded receptively to Philip's message and filled their world with joy.

Even though Stephen is a victim of violence, God uses his stoning as a catalyst to send Philip to fulfill Acts 1:8 in Samaria. Ironically, it is the people who are on the border between Jewish and Gentile regions who respond together to the gospel, and the city is filled with joy.

Author Jennifer Senior writes about a study conducted by George Valliant. He followed the same group of Harvard sophomores from 1939 and collected data for each one. By analyzing Valliant's findings, Senior discovered that the difference between fulfilled and unfulfilled lives was the joy that these graduates exhibited. She writes:

> Their lives were too human for science. Too beautiful for numbers, too sad for diagnosis, and too immortal for bound journals. Joy comes from attachment. Joy is connection. The other kind, happiness, turns the individual inward, which the second turns the individual outward toward others. It's about watching your grandmother and brother chase you. It's a bond that says I want to be connected with you at Thanksgiving. Joy is about being warm, not hot. Excitement, ecstasy and happiness all speed up the heart; joy and cuddling slow the heart down.[1]

Two Kinds of Unity

Just as Jerusalem and Samaria experienced two contrasting ways to be united, Christian groups experience the same tension. When unity is the end, any group can quickly devolve into misbehavior. Sunday school, small groups, and parachurch studies can easily become nests for victimization, gossip, and real or imagined enemies. Jerusalem was an example of this kind of group—a closed group. Christian groups can also unite for a common pursuit. They can repeatedly be open to the movement of the gospel. Samaria was an example of an open group. The difference happens by intentionally reminding the group to be open to God's movement. Let's notice the difference.

Open vs. Closed Groups

Open	Closed
Warm	Hot
Connects	Divides
Slow	Fast
Others	Me
Converts	Confuses
Unites around a Common Pursuit	Pursues Unity
Church	Mob
Joy	Revenge

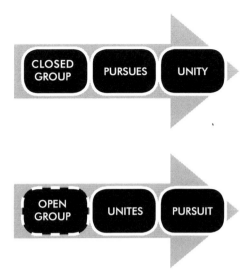

In Jerusalem, the group's unity was the end. They just wanted to stay together, and they did whatever it took to eliminate a rabble-rousing deacon of the church.

Philip and the Samaritans looked outwardly. He was not looking for unity as the ultimate end. He wanted people to unite so they could accomplish their pursuit of the gospel wherever it took them, so he went where Jesus told him. His mission caused him to scatter, and it took him first to Jerusalem and then Samaria. Philip wanted all of them to be a part of the mission too. He explained to them what he was pursuing: the power of God in their lives. The Samaritans were actually his focus. Philip turned his community outward and said, "I want you, the ones who rejected the disciples before." Philip exemplified what the Samaritans wanted for their city. Their community connected together in a common pursuit beyond themselves. They wanted their whole city to be filled with the same connection they had to Phillip.

The Jewish leaders of Jerusalem were all about preserving their community. Their purpose was only for the community. The Samaritans unified and connected to each other so they could experience the power of God. Like a thermos, you can preserve whatever is boiling in your life, or you can use whatever is inside you as an opportunity to invite others in for a common pursuit.

I can usually tell a lot about a person's life just by asking how they are enjoying their church family. Are they connecting? Do they enjoy being here and coming to worship? Because when you are complaining, you are not on mission, and if you leave frustrated, you are traveling down the inward road. But when we turn outward and start talking about the needs of others, and when a person like Philip shows up and starts pointing people to the power of God, something happens that is so magical. It is almost as if God is here—because God is.

Let me give you just one example. When we moved to Knoxville ten years ago, Joe was the retired principal of my son Parker's elementary school. When we moved there, Joe worked behind the scenes to make sure Parker got the best kindergarten teacher at the school. He was very active in the life of our church. His wife, Mary Ann, was a member and a deacon, and she was on my search committee. Joe was not a Christian or a member of the church. Joe was Jewish. His family had encouraged him to be a rabbi, but Joe chose a different path. When Mary Ann gave birth to their daughter, they decided to raise her with the freedom to choose between Judaism and Christianity. She visited synagogues and churches. She joined the youth group, chose Christ, and Joe decided to continue to come to church.

When Joe retired, he said, "All my life I've been focusing on other people. I've been a principal at a school, I've served, I've taken care of everyone else's needs; now I need to focus on me."

That might seem a rather odd sort of statement to make, but Joe always pursued others and never took the time to think through the eternal implications for himself personally. When he retired, Joe volunteered at the church—he worked the front desk as a greeter. Occasionally Joe would say to me, "We need to talk." He came to prayer meeting, asked questions, and read N. T. Wright's book *Simply Christian*.

He asked me about grace, law, obedience, and duty. One day, Joe said, "I'm ready."

"Ready for what?" I asked.

"Ready to take the next step," Joe replied.

Joe made an appointment and prayed to receive Jesus Christ as his Lord and Savior. I said, "Joe you've been coming to church a long time. You've been witnessed to by every pastor, every schoolteacher, every person you can imagine. What made the difference?"

Joe replied, "The church just let me be me. The church let me belong here, serve here, and just be here, and you've shown by your lives what kind of Christ that you serve. I've seen it demonstrated, and now I'm ready to do the same."

That night I celebrated with Joe's wife and daughter that Joe had finally found his joy.

What is your common pursuit, your mission that can lead others to the joy of your life?

NOTE

1. Jennifer Senior, *All Joy and No Fun: The Paradox of Modern Parenthood* (New York: Ecco, 2015), Kindle edition.

11

Someone Has to Be First

Acts 8:9–40

The early church was full of firsts. The first disciple added to the twelve, replacing Judas: Matthias. The first deacon: Stephen. The first miracle performed by an apostle after the resurrection: the lame man healed by Peter. The first missionary to leave Jerusalem: Philip.

Two missionaries receive relatively little publicity by the church. Yet without their work, the gospel would not have spread. The first of these people is Philip; the second is Ananias. The works of both missionaries are hinges that open the door for the Way. The stories of these two missionaries remind you of everything that has been accomplished thus far in the formation of the church, and they prepare you for the unhindered gospel that is to come. They exemplify the complexity of community. Evangelism is not simple, and the people we encounter are fascinating characters and case studies. These stories reveal the adventurous nature of faith.

Life in Philip's House

Think for a moment what it might have been like in Philip's house.[1] Philip was a Greek-speaking Jewish man. He lived in a different area of first-century Jerusalem and took care of his people differently than the Hebrew- and Aramaic-speaking Jews who shared the same town. No sooner did the Way start to gain converts than some of Philip's fellow Greeks argued about the services they received from the Way. Philip and his good buddy Stephen were appointed by the Holy Spirit and the people to take care of these issues. They were the "Wednesday night supper" waiters and servers. They took care of the needy. There are only two deacons in Acts that we ever hear about again: these two, Stephen and Philip. Everywhere they go issues arise, and the doors to the gospel close behind them. They must keep walking forward.

Their experience reminds me of something Parker Palmer describes in his book *Let Your Life Speak*. When discerning God's will, we often think that God tells us what to do by looking forward. A door will miraculously open that we had not expected. However, just the opposite happens to Philip and many other people. Palmer works from within a Quaker tradition that says people discover the way forward by paying attention to the "way closing behind."[2] Philip and Stephen become deacons because of problems in the Jerusalem church. Philip leaves Jerusalem because of Stephen's persecution and the subsequent arrests that occur. Philip sees what could have happened, looks at the doors closing behind him in life and the issues that could have arisen. That's when he knows he did something right.

My long time mentor and friend Dr. Brian L. Harbour once told me that he did not know for sure what the next step was in life until he left one place, went to the next, turned around, and realized there was no going back. Only then did he know if the new place was where God was calling him to be.

My guess is that Philip only realizes that the Spirit has blown him through the winds of persecution to Samaria when he sees that he could have been stoned. Gratefully, he obeys God's direction.

First to Samaria (with Some Help)

Someone had to be first to move out of Jerusalem and into Samaria. Someone had to take Jesus up on his challenge to go into uncharted territory. The disciples waited until there was nowhere else they could go in Jerusalem, then Philip finds himself in the place that was once closed off to disciples—Samaria.

Philip is the first evangelist to go into the territory following the resurrection. While there, the remarkable happens. As I mentioned in my last sermon, Simon, the village's magician, viewed the miracles, signs, and wonders of Jesus as a commodity to be bought and sold. As Charles Talbert suggests, "Magicians looked for customers not converts."[3]

The same thing happens in religion. There is always a church or a temple down the street that draws a crowd just as honey draws flies. Usually the symbol of the group is the person behind the magic. The people, as they say, were drawn to him. The brand might be magic, but everyone came back talking about Simon. There is always a get-out-of-debt-quick solution, a reverse mortgage for sale, a simple fix for everything. And when you mix in Jesus, it can be quite demonic. This is the first time "Jesus" was used as an adjective.

Philip intercedes, albeit with some limitations. He decides to introduce Simon to Jesus, a plan that suits the magician just fine. He is even baptized, but there is one thing lacking. Simon has not received the Holy Spirit. In fact, Peter and John, functioning as a kind of two-man appellate court panel, are following now in Philip's footsteps to check things out. Because Simon has not yet received the Holy Spirit, Peter and John lay their hands on him to complete the process. To make matters worse, we are still not sure if Simon converted. He wanted to pay Peter and John for their spiritual powers. He still does not understand. When confronted, lest what happened to Ananias and Sapphira happen to him as well, Simon asks for prayer so he does not die.

This scene raises a lot of questions for me. I wonder if he is unwilling to repent of his previous work in magic. Why does Philip's baptism require the services of Peter and John? Is there something incomplete? Or is the gospel a little more complicated than we want to admit? The gospel includes everyone, and it takes more than just inclusivity to make it happen. The gospel is open to all people, but it takes more than just openness and outward focus for the gospel to take root. Philip can be open to a magician, but the magician has to change as well. God can use Philip, but Philip also needs help from Peter and John.

Life is not always based on a simple formula. When the Spirit and the gospel break through boundaries, God also breaks through the way we think things are going to happen. He knows that moving forward also entails seeing the door shutting behind us.

The last time the disciples were here, all they could do was shake the dust off their feet. Now, with Simon, just as soon as we are ready for him to be carted off like Ananias, he is alive and asking for prayer. He will not die like Herod and Sapphira.

First on the Road to Gaza

When we have pondered Simon's apparent reprieve long enough, an angel of the Lord intervenes. The Spirit spoke to Philip again audibly and told him to go to the desert. As Dennis Smith describes, "It was a strange command, like it came from a heavenly travel agent or something. And what a choice for a journey! Why go there of all places, on a desert road."[4]

I can imagine Philip wondering, "God, don't you need me where I'm popular—don't you need me where they speak my language?"

In the middle of the desert, down the road from Gaza, Philip confronts another first in his life. He is one of the first deacons, he is the first to go to Samaria, and he is about to be the first to do something else.

Before he looks for an oasis in the desert, he sees a cloud of dust in the distance. He sees a middle-eastern carriage—what some would call a chariot. A dark-skinned man rides along. Philip hears the voice again.

"Great!" Philip likely thought to himself, "It's a God-fearer, someone who is a Gentile following the Jewish law."

By the time he reaches the chariot, he's realized this is no ordinary man. This is an Ethiopian. He is from one of the most exotic places in the world, but he is a man who was considered unclean by some of the Jewish people. If magicians were not trouble enough for the gospel, Philip now encounters none other than a eunuch from the area today known as Sudan.

People in antiquity believed that ancient Ethiopia was located in the farthest reaches of the world. Ethiopia was the "uttermost parts of the earth" (Acts 1:8). Instead of Philip having to go to the "uttermost," those "parts" have come to him.

Even though this eunuch was a highly regarded treasurer in the court of the queen of the ancient kingdom of the Ethiopians, there was no way on earth, according to Deuteronomy 23, that a man like this would be admitted into the temple. Ethiopians, in addition to their dark complexion, would have likely been ritually castrated at birth because of their slave status, and many were mutilated as children. They were strange characters, viewed primarily as both men and women, who were generally subjects of doubt, gossip, and speculation in Philip's day. Out in the middle of nowhere, the Spirit has decided to find this man.

You can imagine the eunuch would have been accompanied by an entourage. Philip would have hardly gone unnoticed by the entire group, but would certainly have gone unnoticed by the eunuch. The official is consumed by reading. Why would he not pay attention to Phillip? More than likely, he was reading out loud (v. 30). In fact, Philip uses a play on words to ask him a question. Literally, he says, "Do you know what you're trying to know?" Most people required the services of some kind of assistant in order to read. Reading was a communal act.

The eunuch is reading from the version of the Old Testament that Jesus used, the Greek translation called the Septuagint. His passage was from Isaiah 53, about the Suffering Servant.

Now let's review. Earlier in chapter 8, Samaritans who were rejected because of their intermarriage and failure to worship at the temple are being introduced to the Messiah. The Spirit overcomes geography, ethnicity, and commercialization to get to them.

On the road to Gaza, the Spirit crosses racial, ethnic, and bodily boundaries to reach a man at the height of political power in ancient Ethiopia but who had been left out of the religious world that he so desired to share.

Philip is confronted with the last barrier he has to cross, the barrier that has plagued the Jewish people and is now the invitation to believers: will you cross the boundaries of sin and prejudice against persons who are outcasts?

Why would an Ethiopian eunuch be such a test case for this Greek-speaking Jewish person? He represents everything that Jesus confronted in the old religious systems. A person could be wealthy materially but an outcast spiritually.

The Ethiopian was one of the wealthiest men in the world, the treasurer for a queen. (You pay your treasurer well so he is not tempted to steal from the treasury.) He is also one of the most maligned men in the world. Sexually and physically, he is an outcast—a eunuch. He is rejected by society, and he is also rejected from the mainstream Jewish religion, which according to Deuteronomy said that you couldn't have eunuchs in the temple because they were viewed as sexually impure.

In the "safe confines" of the desert, Philip overcame all his prejudices—those things he had been told about eunuchs and foreigners while growing up—and simply told the story of Jesus. Someone had to be first, and Philip was the first to say, "I will go to the people we have been taught to avoid our whole lives. I will share the good news with this man." Philip is the first to have the courage to talk to a Gentile about the Lord.

The hardest boundaries in life to cross are not the borders of nations or neighborhoods; they are the boundaries we erect in our own hearts. We continue to set up barriers today, as we have been taught there are certain people we just do not hang out with. Those boundaries are crossed one relationship at a time.

If we are ever going to share the gospel—if we are going to be Christ's light to the world—it requires our willingness to say, "There is no desert that I would be unwilling to cross to share this message with you." Because the gospel is inclusive, someone like you is often the first one in the family of faith to do it.

The First Interpreter

What are we responsible for when God breaks through boundaries? We are responsible for moving forward when the way closes behind us, to be faithful to interpret the Scriptures, to bless those who God sends our way, and to move on when necessary. Someone has to be the first to take this journey. Someone is about to join you on the road, someone like a eunuch, an untouchable in our society. The journey is your chance to be the presence and the love of Christ to that friend or neighbor.

Philip's role is to be the first interpreter. He interprets by his life and lifestyle what he is to do. Philip is not called to change Simon or the eunuch; he is called to join them, talk with them, and explain the story of Jesus to them. When he needs help, he calls in reinforcements: Peter and John. He blesses Simon through the laying on of hands. He joins the Ethiopian on the desert road and interprets the Scriptures. But then someone also has to respond to the gospel, and that's where Simon and the eunuch come in.

The best sermon you will preach to our world will be the one you preach to your peers. By challenging them to reach out to the unlovable, to touch the untouchable, to share with those whom others neglect, you will give the best testimony of your life to those around you about who Jesus really is. And whether or not you are first, there's always a first time for everything.

The reality is, Philip might have been the first to do it all, but he had the Holy Spirit to go before him and pave the way. We are not pioneers; we are just willing to do what others have already done. They have taken the risks, they have stepped out in faith, and they have broken down the boundaries.

Remember this started with a deacon willing to pick up a dinner napkin and serve some people in his church. Then persecution broke out. The rest is what the book of actions is all about.

Philip goes to two places on the margins of society to demonstrate to us the boundless work of the gospel. It breaks boundaries through its work and offers repentance to anyone who responds.

Now what could Acts be teaching us today about the power of the Spirit as we form the Common Way here?

Both Simon and the eunuch attempted to understand the gospel, but both needed assistance. Philip shared the gospel, but he needed assistance. Both the eunuch and Simon were baptized, but only one was someone that we think, "Wow, that was a real convert." Simon seems to be looking for monetary gain, but the eunuch goes home rejoicing. It is the work of the same apostle, and only one seems to make it.

The Spirit uses Scripture, Philip, and the recipient to do its work. Philip blesses the person as they are. He baptizes the person in Jesus' name. Philip receives whomever the Spirit sends to him or sends him to. He explains what he knows and receives help from others. The Scripture testifies on his behalf. The recipient repents.

We cannot convert without help from others and the gift of the Spirit. Simon needs Philip's instruction and Peter and John's gesture. Simon needed someone to publicly validate that he was legitimate. They needed the gesture of the laying on of hands for the Spirit to be received. The eunuch needed assistance reading and interpreting.

The church becomes the interpreter for the world in the same way that Jesus was the interpreter in the Old Testament. The church interprets, through the power of the Spirit, what the Bible says to the world. This gathering of believers is where the Bible, the Spirit, and the people come together.

Both Simon and the eunuch needed to respond to the gospel, but only one did. The gospel is inclusive, but it is also contingent on a response. The imperative of the gospel demands a response of repentance. The gift of interpretation motivates a willingness to change. Simon did not, but the eunuch did.

When comparing these passages, we might ask if baptism delivered the Spirit to the eunuch. No, baptism does not deliver the Spirit; baptism is simply the sign of the Spirit's presence in the process. The Spirit compels Philip to go to both places. Peter and John are ushered in to complete the process. Acts thickens the process a bit to demonstrate the complex nature of what's going on here. We have one act split into several parts, but it is also considered one act. In the eunuch's case, you have several acts combined into one fabulous moment in his life.[5]

The question for us today is not: why isn't the Spirit present in the baptism of Simon? We also should not focus on what is present at the baptism of the eunuch. Our question is: how does the church demonstrate a community that reflects this mission?

The gospel can break through faith healers, self-gurus, the sexually impure, and the personally repulsive. It is all possible. It can also break through the boundaries of the missionaries too. The inclusiveness of the gospel comes with a demand that is often overlooked. Repentance is part of the process. A gift requires response. We must receive, and the way we receive is how we live.

Maybe that is why Philip is there, to serve the greater purpose of the mission. Many of you have had to deal with people who turn to all sorts of remedies to cure what ails, but our job is to be in service of the greater mission, let the Spirit work on its response, but let nothing hinder you from sharing the good news of the gospel.

NOTES

1. Philip the apostle, mentioned in Acts 1, is different than Philip the deacon of Acts 6 and 8. Philip the deacon leaves because of threats to the apostles.

2. Parker Palmer, *Let Your Life Speak: Listening for the Voice of Vocation* (San Francisco: Jossey-Bass, 2000), 37–38.

3. Charles H. Talbert, *Reading Acts: A Literary and Theological Commentary*, Reading the New Testament (New York: Crossroad, 1997), 85.

4. Michael E. Williams and Dennis E. Smith, eds., *Acts of the Apostles*, vol. 12 of *The Storyteller's Companion to the Bible* (Nashville: Abingdon Press, 1999), 70.

5. Charles H. Talbert, *Reading Acts: A Literary and Theological Commentary on the Acts of the Apostles*, Reading the New Testament (Macon GA: Smyth & Helwys, 2005), 86–87.

12

A Place Called Home

Acts 9:1–31

How did you get here today? Not physically here but spiritually *here*? Acts attests to two ways. One way is by a tradition passed onto you from one person to another. A disciple leads another disciple to Christ either through friendship or daily interaction. Another way is through a direct encounter with Jesus. Both require *koinonia*, or fellowship. Both require communities to embrace, support, test, encourage, and hold individuals accountable.

Community is the group where traditions and experiences come together. We experience and revisit what we do and how these people hold us together in the midst of fears—even when our lives have not matched up to Jesus' words.

Acts 9 describes four conversions: the transformations of two disciples and two religious centers. The Spirit converts Ananias and Saul as well as their home bases of Jerusalem and Damascus. In the course of this conversion process, Ananias and Saul begin to deal with what these changes mean. They discover that tradition and experience collide. When this collision happens, we need God to intervene and teach us a new definition of holiness and a way to face our fears. Eventually, God sends us to the place where we came from, back home on a mission.

Fellowship of Fear (9:1-14)

Damascus believers. Just 135 miles northeast of the disciples' home base in Jerusalem was a fellowship in a desert of misdeeds. While the disciples struggled with the Jewish leadership down in Jerusalem, a small group of the faithful was beginning to meet in the town of Damascus. It was like an oasis for them in many ways.

But rumors are circulating that the Jewish leadership was now actually arresting Jewish people. Deacons like Stephen had been stoned in broad daylight while Pharisees and their students took notes on the technique, actually condoning this violence after a synagogue meeting. To make matters worse, people were now saying that the chief priests were enlisting some of the most zealous leaders to root out the problem in Damascus.

People wondered, "Why can't the Pharisees leave them alone? It was just a small group of people; couldn't they just let the Jesus-followers go about their business?"

Rumors were flying, and problems were surfacing. One of the leaders of that band of disciples in Damascus, named Ananias, was having a terrible night's sleep.

Converting Ananias. He lived just outside of Damascus. Going down to Straight Street to worship with fellow believers, he had been up all night worried about his family. Some of the women had arrived saying that Saul, one of the most ardent Pharisees of all, was about a day's journey away. Saul intended to meet with the leaders of the synagogue who lived in that part of Damascus. Saul was planning to arrest people in their Sabbath service. The fellowship of disciples in Damascus suddenly turned into a fellowship of fear.

The rabble of the rumor mill can cause all sorts of anxiety, especially when we listen. The world is full of rumors, wars, and rumors of wars (Matthew 24:6; Mark 13:7). Destructive values lead to infighting, which leads to immoral choices, which lead to worries.

We are much more likely to be swayed by an email with no source citations than a credible professor who speaks on the same topic. Gossip is quick and shocking, and our emotions can more easily adjust our thinking than reason. A thorough explanation is probably long-winded and logical, if not dull.

I imagine that these circumstances raise Ananias's anxiety level to a fever pitch. Up all night, worried, wringing his hands, praying, even worried praying, he's thinking that his very life might be at stake.

What causes this type of anxiety that Ananias confronts? We are actually deeply afraid of outsiders and behave self-righteously toward those who oppose us. If anyone poses a threat, the easiest defense is to start rumors about him. Another defense is to create false opponents and scapegoats.

Suddenly, Saul is going to become the bad guy. He is the scapegoat of the Damascus believers' problems. It is us versus Saul. It is us versus the Israelites. It is us versus any other religion. We forget that their religion and their behavior are not our problem. We are the problem, and sin is the problem.

The rabble of rumors is God's alert system that God is about to move. Before Joshua entered the promised land, rumors spread: "You know what they say about the promised land? There are giants over there!" When Ruth walked into Bethlehem, they whispered about her. I'm sure the same was said about the Samaritan woman in John 4 and the adulterous woman in John 8.

Ananias's Vision of Holiness (9:15-19)

That is when it happened. Ananias thinks he is hearing God speak to him. The text literally reads, "God spoke in a vision" (9:12). This is an "auditory vision" or an "audition."

Ananias's protests begins, "Lord you know what they say about him; you know what the word on the street is." He tries to answer with the rumor mill, by making the people in Jerusalem more sanctified than Saul. (Notice he calls the people in Jerusalem "saints.")

Redefines holiness. The Lord answers Ananias's protests by changing his definition of holiness. By God's standards, holiness is not a location; it is a mission. It is not a privilege; it is a purpose. He wants Ananias to cut through the worry and just go. Holiness is action and behavior rather than rumor and suggestion. He needs to go down the street a few blocks to welcome a new member.

The people in Jerusalem are not saints because they started to withdraw from the world, hoping that God would kill off the bad people. They are saints because they follow the Lord's leadership and do what they are supposed to do. Their holiness is not defined by their withdrawal or separation; their holiness is defined by getting their feet wet and their hands dirty with the very people who want to kill them. That is why they are truly holy.

Holiness is not "us versus them". It is us, all of us, needing Christ. The only way we can do that is to demonstrate a different lifestyle amid other sectarian groups and cultures. Christian holiness has been solely defined as distinctiveness from others. If our distinctiveness is the only facet of our holiness, then we are little more than a self-righteous sectarian group. Holiness without mission is sectarianism. Mission without distinctiveness is just community service. Holiness combined with mission is transforming evangelism.

Our mistake is that when we see immorality, greed, injustice, and evil, we say, "Let's be holy. We'll go have a longer quiet time, attend an extra church service, retreat with Christian friends, turn up our Christian radio station, and send out twenty fliers about the church service. We could add those folks to the 'prayer list.' But we would not want to be seen with them; we might be a 'stumbling block' to someone else." All this in the name of holiness.

That is not holiness. That is self-righteousness. The only thing self-righteous people do is raise their anxiety. Ananias learns that if he stays huddled away in his synagogue and house church in Damascus, all he has done is just become a worrywart. If he goes, maybe God would involve him in the church.

Holiness not only means that we go on mission, we also go with a vision of Christ's eventual work in that person. Ananias's anxiety falls away when he realizes that Saul's past is not going to predict the present. The future work of Christ in a person's life predicts the present.

Christ travels to Judas's home. He embraces Saul with hand and mouth. When he touches him, the scales fall off Saul's eyes. Christ lays his hands on him, then speaks a word of fellowship, "Brother Saul." Saul is filled with the Holy Spirit and a new light shines in his life.

The other part of the story is just as miraculous. God precedes Ananias. While God tells Ananias to go, he tells Saul to do the same. He had already appeared to Saul on the road. As Saul prays, Christ tells him, "Don't worry, a man's going to come and talk to you and pray with you. You are going to be all right—no worries, no revenge, no heartache, no imprisonment, just embrace, just release from your blindness."

Once Ananias changes this one idea of "us versus them" to "us and them," something else happens. He realizes that the Damascus church actually needs Saul as much as or more than Saul needs them. They need someone with influence; they need his scriptural training; they need his background, public speaking ability, and willingness to listen to God.

We actually need people who are lost, who are sinners, and who hate us. I know that runs contrary to everything we have been taught. But through the eyes of Christ and the powerful transforming work that can be accomplished, we might see something happen. We can see change begin. We can see lives renewed.

When Ananias says "Brother Saul," Paul learns something he would write about much later to the Philippian church. He explained, "Be anxious for nothing—don't worry—but in everything by prayer and supplication with thanksgiving present your requests to God—and the peace of God which surpasses all understanding will guard your hearts and minds in Christ Jesus" (4:6-7).

We usually think of this story in the Bible as the conversion of Saul, but I have a new title for it. I think it is as much about the conversion of Ananias. After all, there is a little bit of Ananias in all of us. When we are overcome by the peace of God filling our hearts, there is no telling to whom we might go.

Converting the Fellowship (9:19-31)

The hardest part is yet to come. Ananias now incorporates Saul into the fellowship of fear. Saul has a traditional Jewish upbringing, but it took a journey to Damascus with the intent to persecute disciples to get to him. Jesus got to him—literally. Not all of us have visions of Jesus, but Saul does. And lo and behold we find him right in the den with people who should be against him—the people who should be afraid of him.

You could find them just down the road on Straight Street in the Jewish district, but they are called disciples. How they got there, we do not know. Who told them about Jesus, we are not sure. Like a lot of Christians in dark corners of the world, we are not sure what or who spoke to them, and Saul does not know these things about them either. The only thing that incorporates him in the community is what we call fellowship. Just as the definition of holiness changes, so does the definition of community. It's a mixed bunch with converts, new people, and folks you are going to test out for a while.

Saul begins to testify, and they test him through role modeling, mentoring, and hospitality. For most believers, the Spirit of God works through behaviors that embrace new believers. And since we know so little about the people in Damascus—the very ones Saul was sent to persecute—I think we have to pay attention to the basket.

The basket had become so symbolic of provision for the disciples in the Gospel of Luke. The basket is a living portrait of the idea that when things are scarce, they had enough leftovers to fill up a basket. When the money ran out, or the food was gone, or they were in a desert place, Jesus provided. How did they know it? They had an example. A kid brings five loaves and two fish, and Jesus provides. Now that is a lot more than a generous moment of God.

The Spirit converts the community by lowering their fears, listening to Barnabas, and rewriting the story of Saul. We are called to fellowship as believers. We cannot go it alone; we cannot do it alone. Just as breathing is to the body, so too do we need each other. But there is always a question of how we do that beyond the punch bowl, the friendly factor, the greeting and hello. Fellowship is more than name tags and handshakes; it is deep-seated accountability to and for each other. And we see how the early churches confronted that with their own worst fears.

Lower their fears. Jesus teaches his disciples that fear can become a barrier to fellowship. After a long, hot day of Jesus' teaching, they are fixated on financial and physical needs. They look at each other, saying, "You take care of it; it is your fault. It's your issue, you need to do this. You forgot the bread? No, you are supposed to do that." So from the outside, a boy comes and he gives them everything they need. The rest Jesus divides.

In our world today, we are naturally afraid. Most Christians don't wait for a search warrant to be issued; we only have to be spooked by a rumor, suggestion, or problem in the neighborhood before we want to go add a set of padlocks on the doors. Under normal circumstances, we would avoid the rumors, spread them, bury them, or attack them.

Resurrection causes as many problems as it solves. One such problem is internal. Resurrection really will not allow us to avoid our fears any longer. In fact, as writer William Willimon says, discipleship often involves "problems which we would gladly have avoided if God had left us to our own devices."[1]

When it comes to fear, normally we would just avoid people like Saul, or build our entire world around the fear of newcomers or the fear of the religious Jews. But discipleship turns us back to the very things and people we are afraid of and asks if you would, literally and figuratively, put them in God's basket.

Listen to an advocate. Just imagine what listening does to a church. A few words here and there, and suddenly we are not afraid of the outside world. No, we are afraid of our own committees. We are afraid of the people we know the best. We are afraid of being afraid. But because we live not on a board but in a church, and now that we are in a community, suddenly the Spirit says to us, "Hey, we are different. We cannot just let this lie."

Think about those Jewish believers who we are being intimidated by other friends. The Damascus disciples choose, instead of fear, to lower the person they are afraid of into a basket. Like the disciples who pick up leftover pieces of bread and filled baskets, now Saul is a source of provision for the disciples. They send Saul out the door, lower him into the basket, and, of all things, he goes to Jerusalem, right into the heart of fear.

For a politician, this would be the equivalent of going from a state capitol to Washington, DC. For a church person, this is like going straight into the heart of whatever barrier hinders fellowship. Saul knows what he was getting into, and were it not for an encourager like Barnabas, he would have never gotten through it.

But if unnamed, unknown disciples could welcome Saul, could not the believers of Jerusalem, who were deeply afraid, also welcome Saul? Only if they will put their fears in a basket.

Rewrite the story. During the 2010 Olympics, I read an interesting study about how the United States ski team trains their skiers. They plan for them to crash. They push them to what is commonly known as "the edge." Many skiers, including Olympic gold medalist Bode Miller, learn to embrace the edge. They love that moment where they almost teeter over the brink. But they also learn what to do afterward. Because anyone who has been in an accident like this knows their instinct is, "We'll never do that again." So the ski team has to train to overcome their fear.

That is where psychology comes into play. Coaches and trainers play a little game with the skiers' mind and get them to imagine that harrowing, horrifying moment when they reach the brink and fall over. It is a terrible and often times emotionally exhausting exercise. They do something else with the mind too. They ask the skiers to reimagine that moment but this time, at the brink, they do it right. They ask the skiers to place their fears aside, and this time imagine themselves reaching the point of the crash and getting it right.

They are replacing what could be their fear of failure with a new image of success. As psychologists say, they "replace the old tapes with new tapes." They tape over the old tapes. This is not merely deleting the file. This is taking the old file and rewriting on top of it.

Psychologically, that makes sense. Spiritually, that is called redemption and forgiveness: letting God replay our fears and show us how the Source of all strength will rewrite them.

Acts shows us how Christians record over their old stories. They rewrite the tape. They replay it over and over again. How in the world did we go from Saul the persecutor to Paul of Tarsus? By reminding themselves of this important moment, again and again, early Christians rewrite the script. They keep asking themselves, "How did we get here? We were deeply afraid of this guy. When did that change? Oh, right. When Ananias of Damascus had the courage to put our fears in a basket and believe in the fellowship of this body to take someone strange and redeem him into something new."

Commissioning Home (9:30)

All of us have come from somewhere. The question is where have *you* come from? How'd you get here? And could God be sending you back there?

So my question for you, as you gather around the Communion table, is what or whom are you afraid of? Your fears are very real today. Does he or she or it have a name? Are your fears letting life control you instead of Christ? Doing so is not really worth the price it costs our fellowship. We cannot let fear of each other, outsiders, or the world change what God is already doing—taking the very things we are afraid of and saying, "I think I can use that." If a little boy was unafraid to surrender his fish, and a community of believers is unafraid to accept a person, what will you put in this basket?

All of us have come from somewhere. The early church shows that, even today, everyone has a place called home. Some of us come because we have always been here, and others of us arrive because something happens and now we will never be the same. But all of us come together at this point in order to move forward together, but only after we have put our fears into the basket and lowered them down a wall.

I think the great irony of this text is that Saul had a place where he came from, and the most important missionary journey he had to make was not back to Damascus, or Antioch, or Jerusalem; it was to the place where he'd come from. He had to go back to his momma. You saw it, didn't you? After they had lowered him to the wall and placed their fears into a basket, after Barnabas was willing to walk right beside him to be his advocate, then Saul had his own work to do. For the first time since his conversion, he had to go back to Tarsus to tell his hometown, likely his mother and his father, that life would never be the same (9:30). I cannot imagine what that was like. I know where he came from was not where he was going anymore, because he's been lowered in a basket. Everyone comes from somewhere, and that place is a place that needs the gospel too. A place called home.

NOTE

1. William Willimon, *Acts*, Interpretation (Louisville: John Knox Press, 1988), 83.

13

Holy Spirit Hospitality

Acts 9:32–10:48

From my perspective, the book of Acts is the Holy Spirit's Facebook. When we read and listen to Acts, we see what the early church experienced. We watch what the Holy Spirit did through wind, fire, miracles, stories, and sermons. The book records how the Spirit works through dreams, visions, and meals. Let's look at another example from Acts 9 and 10: On the coast of the Mediterranean Sea, two men just a few miles apart geographically but worlds apart spiritually were about to be introduced to each other through hospitality. Both men would have to cross more boundaries than they ever thought possible. To do so, the Spirit would have to blow them into each other's lives. One is a Gentile who observes Jewish law—a God-fearer. The other is a Jewish disciple changed by the resurrection. In this case, the God-fearer welcomes the disciple and demonstrates Holy Spirit hospitality.

The Spirit Appears in Joppa

We might imagine the book of Acts as a tribute to the church's growth. In many ways, it is not about the church at all, nor is it about the apostles. Acts serves as a biography of the Spirit's work. The Spirit of God breathes into lives and waits for responses. The Spirit has a unique way of picking out people who do not fit into a traditional church directory. For instance, Saul approved of killing followers of the Way. Ananias was a traditional Jewish layman afraid of being killed for visiting Saul. The Ethiopian eunuch was sexually suspect. If you had to put these faces in the church directory, can you imagine the reaction? We do not even have to wonder. Just watch Peter's response.

A seacoast town, Joppa was home to commerce and a new group of followers of the Way. In a place near modern Tel-Aviv, a new apostle, freshly minted from the resurrection, is learning what it means to be sent away from the comforts of home and to be welcomed by strangers. Peter had come to Joppa because Dorcas, one of the leading widows, had died. People lined the town mourning her loss, but Peter was able to heal her by God's power.

Joppa was also special because of Simon, a local who tanned the hides of dead animals. From his office on the seacoast, he stretched the hides to convert them into paper or shoes. According to the law, Jewish people stayed away from tanneries. Touching a skinned animal made a person unclean. A tanner was permanently unclean.

For some reason, the people in Joppa did not label Simon "the tanner." To them, his occupation did not make him unclean. In fact, Simon was the hospitality person in the community and Peter's host during his stay. Because of Simon's hospitality, Peter looked past the animal trophies on the wall and the tanned hides. Through the good graces of Simon, the apostle received hospitality from the people of Joppa.

God's Spirit always meets us where we are. Interestingly, the Spirit does not break down barriers and doors that are miles apart. The Spirit usually opens the next door right in front of you. God rarely pushes you off the spiritual cliff. God asks you to take the next step. For Peter, the next step after Joppa leads to Caesarea.

The Spirit Appears in Caesarea

A few miles away in another seaport town, another man had arrived with great fanfare. The Roman army had dispatched Cornelius to Caesarea. Herod the Great built this city, which served as a home to a palace for the king, a harbor for trade, a jail for prisoners, and the occupational forces that wreaked havoc and terrorized Palestine. No one messed with Cornelius or his cohort. They were known as the "Italian cohort," either sent or personally requested by Rome. They were also foreigners—Gentiles who could command the attention of the native Jews and others by the simple brute power of the sword.

Cornelius, despite how most people saw him, was actually a generous person who took care of the needy. One night while in Caesarea, Cornelius saw a vision in the night from God, assuring Cornelius: "You are welcome. The labels people put on you do not limit you. God is with you. You need to send for a man just a few miles up the coast named Peter. He will come and explain it to you."

Wouldn't you know that God's heavenly travel agent just happens to be making the arrangements again? The Spirit appears again, this time to Peter, who is surrounded by unclean animal skins. Peter sees a vision of an unfolded sheet. The sheet shows the kinds of animals that Simon likely cleaned. The vision calls Peter to realize that, "As you have been welcomed by Simon (a Jewish man no longer unclean because of his occupation), *be welcomed by* someone else you would once have deemed unclean. Be welcomed by a Gentile."

Outsiders Welcome Believers

The Spirit's radical hospitality in Acts causes nonbelievers and God-fearers to welcome believers. The apostles do not solely go to be the nice people welcoming a stranger. Precisely the opposite happens. The Spirit moves nonbelievers to welcome the believers. Ananias has to be welcomed into the place where Saul is staying. The Ethiopian eunuch invites Philip into his chariot. Cornelius welcomes Peter to his table. The apostles go, but ironically, the host is arguably supposed to be the guest.

Cornelius sends for Peter (probably orders him) to come to his house. Peter meets Cornelius on his terms. Peter enters Cornelius's house, shares table with him, and eats his unclean, idolatrous meat.

When we think of Christian hospitality today, we usually think of ourselves as the hosts. As good hosts, we are in charge. Most of the time, we welcome people to our church, we meet them, we talk to them, we are glad they are here, and we send them on the way, hoping they come back.

Of course, there is an inherent danger in that mentality. If we are only the host, greeter, and hand-shaker, we determine who gets invited. We become the editor of the church directory. We determine what faces are remembered and included.

I recall receiving my yearbook at the end of the school year and noticing that the graduating seniors wore regalia prior to graduation. When I joined the yearbook staff as a sophomore in high school, I learned that the staff staged the events ahead of time in order to release the book on time by the end of the year. But I learned another secret. I attended a private school that prided itself on keeping the rules, and they expelled and suspended students throughout the year who crossed the line. The yearbook staff had to edit these disobedient students out. They deleted faces. They printed only the pictures of people whom the administration wanted you to see and remember.

The problem in Acts is that this mode of editing is not how the Holy Spirit works. Christians are quite surprised to see who is included in the directory. Often, it is the very people known for crossing the line who become some of the most welcoming, hospitable people in the world. The ones edited out by religion become some of the greatest evangelists. That only leaves one place for the believer. We must be willing to be placed in the position of guest at the table.

We enter the outside world where we serve others and behave like the kind of people we want others to become. In the process, we might see the Spirit blowing in a direction that God wants *us* to travel.

Seeing the Vision

Admittedly, this perspective is hard for most believers today. We are taught to be very friendly to people who come to our services and programs. We schedule a time for greeting during or after the worship service. Outside the normal church hours, our friends are typically people who share our beliefs and mostly our values. But if we open our eyes, we might begin to see a Cornelius inviting us to dinner.

I once shared this idea with a friend in Mississippi. I was explaining that our church members were beginning a project of getting to know the "Cornelius characters" of their lives. The key to the relationship had to be simply this—we could not invite Cornelius to church immediately. Cornelius had to invite us first. She was quite puzzled where we would find these persons. I shared with her that we started paying attention to people in our world that were generally nice, hospitable, invited us to lunch, and maybe even their homes during holiday or Super Bowl season, but who were not believers. These included office friends, neighbors, coaches, and parent volunteers at our children's school. Cornelius was all around us. Usually these people were God-fearing people who believed there was a God but had not been engaged in Jesus' life.

The risk, of course, is that other religious people might question our motives or be confused by what we are doing. After all, the label of "stumbling block" functions much like the Sabbath laws did for ancient Pharisees. It is an excuse to avoid relationships with others rather than to engage those who need Christianity.

The question that Peter confronted in his own life—and the one we must address—is whether we trust the Spirit enough to open the doors of our hearts. We cannot determine our friendships based on the insecurities of others, but rather on the need for Christian people to be received into homes and to be entrusted with the gospel.

When we realize the Cornelius vision, the host welcoming us through the power of the Spirit will be someone who needs the Spirit the most. Be prepared to pass the fried chicken and update your Facebook friends accordingly.[1]

NOTE

1. This kind of hospitality is also found in Jesus' instructions in Matthew 10:10-12. The host becomes the guest with whom we share the gospel, letting "peace fall on the house." After I preached this sermon, I discovered another resource. Mike Breen's concept of a "Person of Peace" is a wonderful tool to introduce a church to Spirit hospitality. I encourage you to follow his suggestions. Mike Breen, *Leading Missional Communities: Rediscovering the Power of Living on Mission Together* (Pawleys Island SC: 3 Dimension Ministries, 2013), 31–34.

14

Character: Resurrection Discipleship

Acts 11:11–30

When did you become a Christian? Not the moment you were saved, but when did you begin to realize what the Christian life was all about? In his book *The Tipping Point*, Malcolm Gladwell writes that most people need about 10,000 hours to be good at anything. Some scholars have questioned the amount of time, but we know that there are no overnight successes. Even the Beatles needed time to jell. When the band fun. won their Grammy for best new artist of the year for the song, "We Are Young," they told the audience, "We aren't young anymore." Years of training had paid off.

So what happens behind the scenes when you surrender to Christ? When the door of hospitality blows open and Cornelius walks in, what are we going to do with him? It is the process of conversion that takes a believer into the fully formed life of Christ. But when does that happen? In the book of Acts, it happens when you pour your life into someone and they pour into you. We call it discipleship; the secular world calls it character formation. This theme begins in Acts 11 and continues through Acts 15.

Taken Out by Resurrection

In Acts 15:14, James reports to the Jerusalem believers that God has "taken from among the [Gentiles] a people for his name." This process of taking people out of the Gentiles began in Acts 11 with Cornelius's conversion. But the process of transforming people—both Jews and Gentiles—is God's work of taking people out of their current situation, converting them, and forming a church.[1]

As the Spirit calls people, God takes something out of them—their loyalty to the gods and goddesses that control them. They too are taken out or called out to be a different people. The new converts are taught for a year. They call it "the teaching" or the *didache*. For a year, they are educated and resocialized into the practices that constitute a life in the Way.

As the gospel spreads, so does persecution. Ironically, Saul and Barnabas scatter because of the persecution that Saul has instigated. Herod Agrippa I initiates one of the earliest Roman persecutions. Eventually this pressure leads to the death of Jesus' brother James. When Saul and Barnabas arrive in Antioch on the Orontes River, one of the ancient world's largest cities, some of the believers from Cyprus and Cyrene spoke to the Greeks.

When the believers share their faith, it does not matter to the Greeks that Jesus is Lord to the followers of the Way. There were plenty of gods to go around and practices enough to satisfy everyone. For Greeks, Jesus is just one more among many. Luke, however, says Jesus conquers the other gods.

When dealing with American cultures, monotheists like Christians easily forget how difficult it is for our society to follow Jesus exclusively. People are quite often loyal to many gods: material things, weapons, success, athletic teams, and sex just to name a few. Each one has varying degrees of influence on society. Nevertheless, when preaching to our cultures, we must identify the other gods in order to show how they are rivals to the one true God. Antioch shows us how the apostles proclaimed Jesus' Lordship and how the resurrection shaped their character.

Character Formation in Antioch

Converting to "Jesus is Lord." People are turning to Jesus as Lord. They are converting. The resurrection turns people's hearts back to the One who created them. This collection includes people such as the eunuch, Cornelius, and Saul. Wouldn't you know that Barnabas takes Saul from his home of Tarsus and brings him to this place called Antioch?

Antioch becomes a boot camp for the Way. Antioch becomes sort of like a Christian boot camp. It is the place where character formation can happen. Damascus cannot handle Saul; Jerusalem cannot take Saul; but Antioch can.

Barnabas teaches Saul. For a whole year they meet with the church and teach. Now that is not just a small word; it is implied or suggested that there is a teaching or a curriculum—something that formed and shaped the world and lives of these new Christians. This is a lesson series in what we might call character formation.

The community examines Saul. In Antioch, the church is a phenomenon countercultural to the violence and destruction of their world. As people are suffering for their faith, Antioch is the place that sees this suffering as a sign of success. As William Willimon suggests, a group of people behave differently than the cultures around them. Their conduct runs against the grain of everything their city is about. These disciples must be transformed during a season of nurturing that prepares them to be sent out into the world. They need a new language, worldview, pattern of life, and social system. They are trained in love, truth telling, justice, obedience, and reconciliation. They practice their performance of God's word to people who respond immediately with feedback. They provide accountability, encouragement, and mentorship to people like Saul.

If this sounds familiar, it should. The gods we worship in our modern society invite parents to attend all kinds of things early on—basketball camp, dance camp, music camp. Why? The gods must indoctrinate you into their way of life. They show up with the fun and the frolic and all the ways to hook you in, take you out, set you apart, and turn you into some sort of team. We are part of swimming culture; there is a language, a skill set, a dedication, and a code of conduct to learn.

By the time we become adults, those gods mask themselves as vacation destinations, bigger vehicles, and larger homes. Why? Because most gods have a standard of living; most gods have some sort of expectation for you.

I remember talking to a chemist who said that once you decide to join this field, there is an expectation that you are going to judge each other's work. You are expected to look for problems in theories and experiments. No one keeps their ideas to themselves because chemists need other scientists to explain the things that are wrong in order to make their work even better.

Social workers have field training. Physicians have residencies. Marines have boot camp. The 2012 book, *SEAL Team Six: Memoirs of an Elite Navy SEAL Sniper,* discussed the intensity of Navy SEAL training. Their training alone gives us a glimpse of what we are trying to do as believers. Authors Howard Wasdin and Stephen Templin reported what one Navy SEAL had to say about the most intense part of the training, known as "The Week":

> Deprived of support in our environment and the support of our own
> bodies, the only thing propping us up was our belief in accomplishing

the mission—complete The Week. In psychology this belief is called
self-efficacy. Even when the mission seems impossible, it is the strength
of our belief that makes success possible. The absence of this belief
guarantees failure. A strong belief in the mission fuels our ability to
focus, put forth effort, and persist. Believing allows us to see the goal
(complete The Week) and break the goal down into more manageable
objectives (one evolution at a time). If the evolution is a boat race, it
can be broken down into even smaller objectives such as paddling.
Believing allows us to seek out strategies to accomplish the objectives,
such as using the larger shoulder muscles to paddle rather than the
smaller forearm muscles. Then, when the race is done, move on to the
next evolution. Thinking too much about what happened and what is
about to happen will wear you down. Live in the moment and take it
one step at a time.[2]

Trainees undergo elite regimens, special instructions, weeks of intense
workouts, and many of those who are trained do not qualify for the task.
But when they are finished, they are part of a new culture. What happened?
They are separated from others, given a new language, behavior, respect,
community, and then sent out with a whole new mindset. So what about
believers? If a chemist, a Marine, or anyone else is set apart, then why
wouldn't the believers? What is ironic for us is that we usually depend on
college or the Marines or someone else to shape the characteristics that are
so often lacking in what it means to be changed. If believers can change
our habits and routines for six to eight weeks, our habits, memories, and
routines will change.

Recognizing the Difference

Apparently believers did notice a difference in Antioch. Once the church
showed hospitality to people like Cornelius, the transformation began.
Formation follows hospitality. This pattern of life becomes a term coined
by outsiders to describe what they saw of these Christ-followers. They are
called "Christians." In fact, the only time Luke uses the term is in the places
where Gentiles are introduced, which only happens twice: once in Antioch
(11:26) and the second in Paul's trial before Agrippa II (26:28).

It seems to me that the eunuch, Saul, and even Cornelius would have
to go through some sort of boot camp. Acts says that, after Pentecost, they
devoted themselves to bread and prayer. Acts 4 says their corporate life

required worship and giving. So here Barnabas and Saul meet with the church and teach. This nurturing task requires additional leadership so that the tasks at hand can be performed. This allows the believers to vouch for Saul's authenticity and then also to find out if he can really do this. In this way, there is mutual teaching and edification. Saul is going to pour his life into them, and they are going to pour into him. In this way they are becoming Christians.

This is the nature of conversion. As the Reformers said, sin is deeply embedded in our lives and in the culture we live in. The gospel is so demanding and different that only a lifetime of conversion can really change us into the new creations that God has called us to be. Remember, Saul's conversion is reported three times in Acts, and each with attendant confirmations. Even here, there is the sense that a delegation from Jerusalem must come and confirm this change of the Spirit. Why? Because there are no individualistic expressions or "one size fits all" conversions. There is an ongoing process of being changed that comes by the grace of God.

So when did you really become a Christian? I'm not talking about the time you accepted Jesus, punched that card, and jumped in the waters. I'm talking about when Christianity—the name, the title, the moniker—really became noticeable to others through you.

If you asked the people in the book of Acts, for some of them it would have been quick, but for Paul it was three years (based on his experience in Galatia). Everyone was taken and trained and sent out so that they could then be formed into someone we recognize today as a Christian. We can see that evidence in our lives if we just look for it.

Conversion is the evidence of the miraculous power of God to make the church the church and to overcome the enemy and boundary at the very center of the church's life. There are times in my life when I'm like Saul, and there are other times I'm like Barnabas. As I thought about this message, I realized I need someone to pour into me, and I need to pour into someone else.

There is a process of believing, turning, teaching, and character formation. And of all people in our passage, the one changing is the persecutor named Saul. Barnabas retrieves Saul after confirming the work of God, not only to find out if the believers in Antioch are real, but also to find out if Saul is too.

The great irony of all this is it happens when the emperor Herod Agrippa I begin to persecute and scatter the people. Now Saul—the one who had been persecuting—is caught up in it. What do we do when we are in the midst of struggle? Do we fall away or become more devoted to that which we are doing?

This is what it means to form a culture, to be taken out in such a different way that, when we reemerge, we have a whole new way of living. And that is what happens when we gather together.

If you asked most people who say they are active in their faith to count the number of times they are in church on a Sunday morning, most would report one out of every four Sundays. That's what most of us consider active faith now: twenty-five percent attendance, fifty percent among leaders. Why? Because we become very complacent about what it means to be taken aside and socialized into becoming a believer. We come up with excuses for not attending: church was something for the kids. If someone from out of town visits over the weekend, we stay home instead of bringing them to church. Gods can be difficult and jealous at times.

But there was a time, and a time is now appearing again, when believers were so interested in living out the resurrection power in their lives that one thing happened which no one expected. They became Christians.

So where do we start?

1. Convert to Jesus as Lord of all

2. Attend church

3. Learn from a Barnabas

4. Teach a Saul

For twelve months in boot camp in Antioch, the believers gathered, taught, shared, and trained. They trained Saul in what he was doing, and they trained Barnabas, and they trained each other—so much so that the reputation they got was an epithet: oh, there go the little Christs. But that name became a slogan: we are the Christians.

NOTES

1. Kavin Rowe, *World Upside Down: Reading Acts in the Graeco-Roman Age* (New York: Oxford University Press, 2009), 18.

2. Howard Wasdin and Stephen Templin, *SEAL Team Six: Memoirs of an Elite Navy SEAL Sniper* (New York: St. Martin's Press, 2012), 95–96.

15

Prison of Pressure

Acts 12

In his book *Lifesigns*, Henri Nouwen says that most of our world plans and prepares based on the question "What if?"1 What if the stock market collapses? The terrorists attack? I get sick?

These are important questions, but a life continually ordered by wondering "What if?" leaves us afraid. Instead, Christians understand that life is full of contingencies. Christians primarily ask, "How will I respond when suffering happens?" Because we believe that Jesus is Lord, Christians learn to plan their responses to the various pressures of life. The prison is the place where Peter experienced this kind of pressure firsthand and through which the church learns how to respond better to pressure.

Three Kinds of Pressure

In a few short verses, we learn that the early Christians experienced three major forms of pressure: random, internal, and external. Random pressure happens in the famines and natural disasters of life. God doesn't send them, but God suffers with those who experience them. Then there is the internal pressure, struggles between believers over how to follow the Way. Then there is external pressure from outside forces. As Kavin Rowe suggests, pressure is a sign of a thriving Christian community.[2]

Our story begins with random pressure from a famine. First-century Jerusalem is in economic collapse. A prophet named Agabus appears to the Antioch church and announces the event. The Antioch church dispatches Barnabas and Saul with the first "love offering" for another congregation. Historically, this disaster becomes one of the pivotal moments that shapes Christianity.

If that isn't enough, the earliest followers of the Way are already struggling with each other. Wherever two or three are gathered together in Jesus' name, there are usually ten different ways to follow Jesus. The number of churches in today's cities is evidence enough of the diverse expressions of Christianity. The early church is no exception. Their widows struggle with each other over the daily distribution of food (Acts 6), and the leaders struggle over which food the Gentiles should be required to eat (Acts 15).

But the focus of our text is on the one person no one thought they would ever get rid of: Herod. Acts, and its prequel Luke, could easily be titled "The Rise and Fall of the House of Herod." There are five kings named Herod in these two volumes, and the books form an account of these Herodians: Herod the Great, his sons Herod Phillip and Antipas, his grandson Herod Agrippa I, and his great-grandson Herod Agrippa II. The Herod in today's passage is Herod Agrippa I. Not only a master politician, Herod Agrippa I was a manipulator. He liked to create problems, incite riots, and spark wars. Once society or a city was in chaos, the people turned to him for rescue. He picked fights to stay in power. He wove people into his trap by doling out benefits to those he needed to manipulate. Those he hated, he bribed; and those whom he wanted to get rid of, he bought off. He was scandalous.

Herod thought that killing James the brother of John would intimidate and scare the small band of believers. Then he decided to take it a step further. On the week of Passover, presumably a year to the week after Jesus died (and was resurrected), Herod arrested Peter, lead apostle of the Way.

You would think, of course, that Peter and the early church understood that God would protect them. Instead, they assumed the worst, as did Herod.

Learning from Pressure

Herod stationed sixteen soldiers—four squads—around Peter to ensure that he could not escape. Because it was Passover week, Peter had assumed that he was the next one to be executed. Taking off his clothes, he slept in the prison like Jonah on the ship bound for Tarshish.

But we serve a God who breaks through the gates of prison and comes to be with us in our times of suffering. God sends "the angel of the Lord" (v. 7) to rescue Peter. There are two other notable times this angel, or an angel with this title, appears. The first is during the Exodus, when the angel passes over the homes of the Israelites who smeared lamb's blood over the doorposts. The Israelites testified their trust in the Lord, and the Egyptians lost their first-born sons because of their lack of trust. The angel of the Lord also appears at the empty tomb to announce Jesus' resurrection.

When Peter sees the angel, however, he assumes that it's his guardian angel, not the Lord's angel. There was an old Jewish tradition from the first century that each person had his own guardian angel. The guardian angel only appeared to the person at a time of imminent death. If he ever appeared, it would be the sign of death, not life. Instead, the Lord's angel speaks to Peter like a parent, "Get up, put your clothes on."

We pick up Acts 12:11-18 from there. Notice the nuances.[3]

> Then Peter came to himself and said, 'Now I am sure that the Lord has sent *his* angel and rescued me from the hands of Herod and from all that the Jewish people were expecting.' (v. 11)

Notice the emphasis on *his* (God's, not Peter's) angel. You would expect then that the early Christians were gathering, ready for a miracle to occur. Instead, just the opposite happens: the prayer meeting turns into a fear festival.

> As soon as he realized this, he went to the house of Mary, the mother of John whose other name was Mark, where many had gathered and were praying. When he knocked at the outer gate, a maid named Rhoda came to answer. On recognizing Peter's voice, she was so overjoyed that, instead of opening the gate, she ran in and announced that Peter was standing at the gate. (vv. 12-14)

You can tell that this is a wealthy family based on the outer gates and a household servant named Rhoda. She's the first person to recognize the power of Christ in their midst, but does anyone believe her? Hardly.

> They said to her, "You are out of your mind!" But she insisted that it was so. They said, "It is *his* angel." (v. 15)

The early church assumes it is the guardian angel coming for Peter.

> Meanwhile Peter continued knocking; and when they opened the gate, they saw him and were amazed. He motioned to them with his hand to be silent, and described how the Lord had brought him out of the

prison. And he added, "Tell this to James and to the believers." Then he
left and went to another place. (vv. 16-17)

There was such commotion that Peter had to gesture with his hand to get
their attention. And notice, of course, he wants Jesus' brother James to
be the first to hear the news. Now what happens? The angel of the Lord
appears and moves them from the house of fear to the Passover of
protection. Peter is not a new Jonah swallowed by Herod; he is a new
Moses, leading the people out of bondage into a new territory with the
risen Christ. He's fulfilling what Jesus said to him in Matthew 16: "I will
give you the keys to the kingdom of heaven." Peter is now unlocking the
gates and hearts of not only the Herods of the world but also those in the
church.

In the process, the early church learns through experience what not
to do:

1. *Over-spiritualize.* They had the right intention but the wrong
   execution. Their prayer meeting caused them to jump to the wrong
   conclusion instead of leading them to trust in the power of God.

2. *Publicize.* They do not need to draw more attention to themselves
   because of Peter's release, but instead trust that God can see what
   they're going through.

3. *Victimize.* They choose not to turn this into an "us versus them" battle, pitting the church against Herod. Herod is a threat to everyone,
   not just the early church. They know that they face a greater threat:
   the battle that is unseen between principalities and powers.

From Prison to Passover

We serve a God who comes to us in the midst of our suffering, unlocking
even the Christians' barriers of prayer. Peter is locked in Herod's prison; the
Way was held captive by their own fears. God moves us from the prison
of pressure into the Passover of Protection. What does God ask us to do in
the process?

Our Lord invites us to follow Jesus' Passover example. By remembering his suffering, these believers endured with courage and faith. They
were under pressure from outside forces beyond their control. Life is full
of complications, twists and turns. As Kavin Rowe suggests, we suffer in-

nocently and we suffer injustices. Often there is nothing we can do about them. Jesus' response to suffering was not to lash out, strike back, or see what would happen. Instead he endured suffering to bear witness to the power of God's transforming work in that place. On that same Passover week, Jesus suffered and died. Now Passover was an act of memory, and for more than just the Jewish people. For generations, the Israelites had struggled in misery and pain, then God sent Moses to deliver them from bondage. Their deliverance was not just a freedom but also a following of this God into a new place for a new beginning. The early believers had struggled in pain since Christ's death and resurrection. But they saw this moment, Peter's miraculous release from jail, as their Passover. With Peter free, the Way was about to move into a whole new territory for a brand new beginning.

When they remembered Jesus' Passover, they were motivated to reach out to others who were suffering. The Antioch church gave them an example. They reached out to the people of Jerusalem during a time of famine. In disaster relief and recovery, we do the same.

Lastly, the believers rejoiced when given the opportunity to suffer for the Name. They rejoiced that they were chosen to be the ones who would suffer. For those who were undergoing suffering, that was their witness. They didn't have to share it with their lips; their lives were the testimony.

We do this in our society, especially on holidays like Memorial Day. We gather and pay tribute to veterans and fallen soldiers. This holiday goes back to the era of the Civil War. One of the earliest celebrations took place in Charleston, South Carolina. Detachments from the 54th Massachusetts and 34th and 104th United States infantry marched into Charleston at the end of the Civil War. They were all African-American regiments. They gathered at the Washington Race Course and Jockey Club. This place was a prison where some 257 Union soldiers died from mistreatment and disease. Over 10,000 Charlestonians, white missionaries, and school teachers attended. Three thousand black school children carried roses. They turned this prison into a cemetery. They honored their dead, sang patriotic songs, watched soldiers drill, and shared a picnic.[4]

They gave thanks for those who had sacrificed for their freedom. They didn't worry about whether it would happen again. They knew they could not prevent future pressure, whether random, internal, or external. They trusted in the power of their community to respond.

The early church did the same with Passover. They remembered their past suffering, knowing suffering would come again, and they rejoiced in the opportunity to honor the name of Jesus.

NOTES

1. Henri J. M. Nouwen, *Lifesigns: Intimacy, Fecundity, and Ecstasy in Christian Perspective* (Garden City N.Y.: Doubleday, 1986), 15–18.

2. Kavin Rowe and L. Gregory Jones, *Thriving Communities* (Durham: Duke University, 2014), Kindle edition.

3. This text needs to be performed so as to emphasize the nuances in interpretation.

4. David Blight, "Forgetting Why We Remember," *The New York Times*, May 29, 2011. <http://www.nytimes.com/2011/05/30/opinion/30blight.html?pagewanted=all&_r=1> (accessed February 9, 2016).

Part Two

Change in the Cities

Part 1 traced the steps of a burgeoning community in Jerusalem. They learned what it was like to live on the Way with Jesus and offered believers and churches today a mirror. By gazing into their lives, we can compare ourselves to the characteristics of the earliest Christian communities. We are not called to do things exactly as they did in Jerusalem. Instead we are empowered by the same resurrection life in Christ to adapt this message in our context with our community.

Where can we see that kind of work taking place? Acts 13–20 reveals the change that happened in the cities as a result of the resurrection of Jesus. Churches sprang up in cities large and small. In rural towns and metropolitan cities, the church became the stabilizing force that held communities together when civil society was in a state of unrest. These sermons and studies follow the Spirit's movement in Antioch of Syria, Antioch of Pisidia, Lystra, Jerusalem, Philippi, Thessalonica, Athens, Corinth, Troas, and Ephesus. These places become the stage for the gospel to reach new people as well as to teach believers about several critical issues. We'll learn about how worshiping Jesus as Lord changed the people, how self-help and apocalyptic preachers were rejected, how Jesus' baptism is used by missionaries, how testimony and hospitality are important for the gospel witness, and how households shape the faith of families and churches.

As churches transform cities, the gospel grows without limitations.

16

Change in the Cities

Acts 13

When you think about Paul and Barnabas, you usually think about missionary journeys. Acts describes missionary expeditions more than journeys. The Spirit sends them to various cities to change the people. In so doing, the gospel spreads throughout the region.

Acts 13–20 marks the second section of this powerful charter document. The first section, Acts 1–12, describes the Common Way of the earliest believers. In section 2, we learn about the change that comes in the cities as a result of this empowering, Spirit-led, and Spirit-filled mission. In Acts 13, two characters take center stage, both of whom we've already met. The church in Antioch sends Saul and Barnabas to Barnabas's home island and eventually to another Antioch, this one in modern-day Turkey. One place challenges the Roman powers and the other, the Jewish leadership in a Roman region of the world. When confronted, the message not only changes the recipients but also the messengers. Saul takes on a new role, and the Gentiles establish their role in the reception of the gospel.

Commissioning from Antioch of Syria (13:1-3)

In some ways, we could describe Acts 13 as a tale of two Antiochs; the one that was the Seleucid capital of ancient Syria, the other, a Roman outpost in Asia Minor. But the chapter tells a story richer in nuance than that. The change begins in the Antioch church itself. The group is now representative of the diversity of the mission.

Simon was called Niger, the Latin word for "black." Presumably he's from Carthage or North Africa. Lucius, or "Red," is from Cyrene, also a North African outpost. Despite the misery at the hands of Herod the Tetrarch, the gospel has infiltrated the Romans. Manaen is also a part of this group. The scene is a preview of what's to come. The gospel does not view the Roman state as an evil empire like the one in *Star Wars*, which must be overthrown at all costs. Rather, the gospel uses the state in order to accomplish its purposes. In this case, the gospel infiltrates the Romans in order to divide and conquer them. We'll meet another Roman official in just a few verses. Before we do, the Antioch church commissions Saul and Barnabas. They do so through a procedure of fasting, praying, and laying on of hands. It is highly unlikely that this commissioning ceremony was designed to set up a ritual of ordination now carried out by churches. It's simply a gesture, much like the one used by Abraham to bless Isaac or by Moses to signify that Joshua was his successor. It's a public way to indicate that these people are the ones we want to send out as missionaries, as representatives. The Spirit doesn't come in this case because the church laid hands on them. The Spirit sends them now that the church has blessed them (13:3).

Roman Officials in Cyprus (13:4-12)

Their first destination is Barnabas's home island of Cyprus. Along the way, they make two official stops, in Salamis and Paphos. At Paphos, they encounter their first opponent, a magician ironically named Bar-Jesus, or Son of Yeshua. What kind of magic he performs, we're not sure. We do know that his kind is satanic in nature and representative of the dark powers and spiritual division in the world. In this case, Bar-Jesus is a source of divination and fortune-telling associated with Sergius Paulus, a Roman proconsul, probably some sort of retired senator. Acts tells us that he is an intelligent man, but even his information cannot give him everything that he needed. He needs someone with connections to a higher power, so he turns to a magician. I like to think of Bar-Jesus' role as Sergius Paulus's director of political operations. He would have been the modern version of someone who runs the polling data and metrics to help the politicians know what to do and say at the right time to keep themselves in power. Bar-Jesus works his magic. Like political operatives today, who cling to big data to predict the future and to address public policy issues, the magic man in Paphos is afraid he'll lose his grip on power and wants to drive a wedge between Sergius Paulus and Saul and Barnabas.

To reach out to Sergius Paulus, Saul tries a strategy with which he is intimately familiar. He looks at Bar-Jesus and accuses him of "making crooked the straight paths of the Lord." Echoing the message of John the

Baptist, Saul accuses this magician of manipulating the situation. In order to correct him, Saul temporarily blinds him. Saul would know of the powerful effect temporary blindness can have. As he discovered in Acts 9, with the right message and messenger, temporary blindness can lead to salvation. Like Saul, Bar-Jesus had to now be led by the hand, dependent on others. We do not know how long his condition lasted, or what the outcome was, but we do know the effect it had on the Roman official, the apostle, and their companion. Sergius Paulus is astonished and believed. From then on, Saul is known as Paul. The people calls him Paul not after his conversion, but after his first confrontation on his first missionary journey with people who knew Barnabas very well. The same could not be said of John Mark, who returns to Jerusalem.

Synagogue Officials in Antioch of Pisidia (13:13-41)

From Cyprus, after a quick stop along the way, Paul and Barnabas are whisked to Antioch of Pisidia in present-day Turkey. They enter a synagogue and sit down. The ruler of the synagogue invites them to speak. Known as a place of reading, prayer, and debate, the local synagogue would be the natural gathering point for Jewish men and women. Paul's speech here is a template for his future declarations of the gospel. The synagogue ruler invites him to "give any word of exhortation" (v. 15). The nature of this question suggests that Paul is not on trial; this is not a judicial speech. We can learn a bit about the speech by paying attention to the gestures he uses and the structure of the speech itself.

Gestures are explicitly mentioned six times in the book of Acts:

1. 12:17 – Peter's speech after being released from prison

2. 13:16 – Paul's first sermon in Acts

3. 19:33 – Alexander in a rioting crowd

4. 21:40 – Paul's defense on the steps

5. 24:10 – Felix giving permission

6. 26:1 – Paul before Agrippa

This one is simply introduced in the NRSV with "a gesture." The Greek is literally "motioned with his hand," a more accurate rendering. Why does this matter? Different issues called for different gestures. The motion, to alert an audience that you were about to speak, is the standing posture (noted in the text) and two fingers extended with an upraised thumb.

Before we read the speech, let's get a sense of how the speech goes. In modern speeches in America today, we would normally have 2-3 points equally distributed throughout the speech, with a concluding story or challenge. In ancient speech writing, they generally had one point somewhere in the middle of the speech. This speech can be outlined this way.[1]

Introduction/*Exordium* (v. 16)

Narration/*Narratio* (vv. 17-25): Background information, statement of facts, why we're here. God's faithfulness has gotten us here. God has chosen us. Notice the reference to Benjamin; Saul of Tarsus and King Saul were both Benjamites.

Thesis/*Propositio* (v. 26): Argument. The same faithful promise God made to Abraham has now been given to us.

Proofs/*Probatio* (vv. 27-37): Evidence, why this matters. Jesus is the fulfillment of God's faithful promise, but everyone acted out of ignorance. Jesus dies because people were ignorant and collaborated with the Romans. Jesus remains faithful to the mission, and God validates and confirms his work by raising him from the dead.

Conclusion/*Peroratio* (vv. 38-41): Call to action, conclusion.

Now let's read the speech with this in mind. Notice that we'll have a gesture to indicate the change to a new section. We'll also raise or lower our voice to indicate the intensity of the section.

When you read the speech with this kind of outline in mind, you'll notice some significant differences the way we normally read a speech. We can get lost in the background of vv. 17-25 or the proofs of vv. 27-37, so realize the whole point is that God has a promise for us right now. Paul's message invites an immediate response.

Let's take a look at several of Paul's key points:

1. God's faithfulness has brought them this far (v. 17). In Stephen's speech, he accuses one group of Jewish people of rejecting the people

like Joseph and the prophets in their midst. In this case, Paul says that God has worked very hard to remain faithful to the people of Israel and to all the people. For example, God uses Saul as Israel's first king, someone from Paul's own tribe. Even though King Saul was a failure, God remains faithful to them. John the Baptist foretold this rejection of the prophets.

2. The listeners are all children of Abraham, and the message is for them (v. 26). Paul draws on their Abrahamic ties, before Moses and before there was a defined Jewish heritage, to say that God has been working to fulfill this promise for a long time. Now, they are the recipients.

3. The only problem is that the Israelites and God-fearers missed and even killed the very promise of God. Jesus died because people acted out of ignorance (v. 27). Notice that Paul does not refer to Mark's rationale for Jesus' death. Mark says that Jesus died "for their sins." Paul explains that Jesus died because the people, in collaboration with the Romans, killed him. Yet Jesus remains faithfully obedient all the way to the end. His death is not a victory but a tragedy at the hands of ignorant people.

4. The good news is that God vindicates Jesus, confirms his work, and offers forgiveness through the resurrection of the dead. It is right there all along in Psalm 2 and Psalm 16. Emphasizing the word "decay," Paul shows how Jesus is the fulfillment of the promise, not the Mosaic law or the deeds that come with it. God's faithfulness is not fulfilled in a book but in a person, not in deeds but in a son. He is the only way to forgive sins. (vv. 38-39)

5. After Paul's arguments, to reject Jesus now is a sign of foolishness. The invitation comes with a warning: don't turn into a scoffer and risk judgment. (v. 41)

Like so many others, this speech functions as a way of introducing us to Paul. It reveals his character as well as the method by which he is going to approach his mission. It also demonstrates the arrangement of the book of Acts itself. God is going to fulfill his promise by raising up new children of Abraham, overcoming their ignorance, and offering salvation through Christ, who has been raised from the dead. This is Paul's Montgomery Bus

Boycott speech, a standout statement just as word about the movement is beginning to spread. We can learn much from it. But in reality, we don't get the speech only; we also get the reaction and results from it.

The Mission Changes People and Cities (13:42-52)

Some of the people invite Paul and Barnabas to return the next Sabbath. Some want to hear more, others want to put a stop to this. When the next Sabbath comes, the entire city gathers, and these two missionaries face rejection at the hands of other Jewish people. Filled with jealousy and blasphemy, some "contradicted" Paul's words (v. 45). Paul and Barnabas respond by basically saying that this was part of the plan: Jewish people will be given the first opportunity and many more to come, but now Gentiles will officially be welcomed into the movement. Remember that not all Gentiles will receive them either. They will face struggles with Gentiles in Ephesus, for example. But for now, this is an opportunity to explain a new beginning. Instead of letting the rebuffs get under their skin, they use a gesture from Luke 10. Paul and Barnabas shake the dust off their feet, and the Holy Spirit fills them. The Spirit who empowered and sent them to go now fills them.

There is so much that goes into the Spirit's mission. It requires information, vision, dependence, empowerment, and boundaries. Sergius Paulus is intelligent with information but lacks the necessary vision or dependence. Paul has the vision and the Spirit. He and Barnabas need boundaries to keep things from bothering them and to simply trust the Spirit within those boundaries.

Of course people reject them, but interestingly, when they reject them, they judge themselves. God does not preordain their judgment (v. 46). This is an important claim, especially as it involves the plan of God. God's plan involves inviting all people; when we reject him, we are choosing that rejection.

The Jewish people in the cities are given the first opportunity to respond (v. 46), but the Gentiles have been part of the plan all along (v. 48). By using children of Abraham, Paul announces that, before there were Jewish people and Muslim people and Christian people, there were God's people. And all God's people have an invitation to follow Jesus and become Christians.

The Spirit changes the people. Saul becomes Paul. John Mark separates from the group. Sergius Paulus becomes the new Pontius Pilate. The Gentiles are officially a part of the plan. Now we must be responsive to the Spirit, lest we fall into the same trap of perverting the straight ways of the Lord. Bar-Jesus did it, the Jewish people of Antioch Pisidia did as well, and we too can grow out of ignorance.

NOTE

1. Mikeal C. Parsons, *Acts*, Paideia Commentaries on the New Testament (Grand Rapids: Baker Academic, 2008), 193–94.

17

Why Are You Doing This?

Acts 14

Monotheism (worship of one God) was a constant challenge for Jews and a real challenge for Gentiles. When Paul and Barnabas heal a lame man in Lystra, the locals assume that they are gods to be worshiped too. Paul turns the tables—and their lives—around and invites them to repent from this behavior. In so doing, he shows us why we worship Jesus the way we do.

Review and Preview (14:1-6)

Acts 14 opens with a review and preview of what is to come. As in Pisidia, they enter a synagogue and teach. Soon thereafter, the city was divided. This time both Jews and Gentiles attempt to stone Barnabas and Paul, a reminder to all of us that Gentile reactions are often as suspect as Jewish reactions. Such is certainly the case when they arrive in Lystra.

Idolatry of Religious Celebrities in Lystra (14:7-13)

Just down the road from Pisidia was the small rural Roman colony of Lystra. It was made up of largely hardscrabble folks in ancient Galatia, the area we know as southern Turkey. The town was full of Greeks, Romans, and Jews. It wasn't known for much, so when strangers like Paul and Barnabas arrived, they became instant celebrities. Like Jesus in Luke 5:18-26 and Peter in Acts 3:1-9, they healed a lame man. Paul gave him the godlike stare, spoke with a loud voice, and the natives were convinced that this was a god come down in human form. Why? Because Zeus and Hermes had done the very same thing. According to legend, Zeus and Hermes had visited this region as strangers, healed someone, and were welcomed by an elderly couple. Not wanting to make the same mistake twice, and miss a god right in front of them, they called Barnabas and Paul "Zeus and Hermes" (v. 12).

It was a pretty common thing for ancient people to think the gods walked among them disguised as humans. People long to believe and they love to fall over themselves deifying each other and thinking that their favorite person is a god. We especially see this in our idolatry of sports figures, politicians, and celebrities. Whether pagan, Jewish, or Christian, we are eager to deify the people who proclaim our various gods over God.[1]

Take the glorification and downfall of Lance Armstrong. He represented the best of humanity, living strong and overcoming obstacles, the best athlete in the world, until it came to light that he had cheated. It was all a sham. You can also look to the latest Christian celebrity on the soccer pitch or the football field and realize that, many times, we are quick to take Bible verses and post them on our cheeks rather than actually read what the Bible says. Rarely does God appear in the New Testament victoriously making a movie and millions of dollars to go with it. God doesn't want much to do with that lifestyle, and neither does Paul.

Compare Lance Armstrong's life to two Christian coaches I have met. One is David Cutcliffe and the other Cuonzo Martin. I invited both of them to speak in our worship services. I was hesitant to do so because I do not like to turn people into celebrities, and I do not like to play the "celebrity at church" game. Many pastors have artificially inflated their attendance numbers with a regular run of popular figures. I intentionally asked these two because they were not on the fame circuit, and I knew a bit of their background.

When I asked Coach Cutcliffe to come, he asked me, "What time do you have your service?"

I said, "Eleven o'clock."

He replied, "Good, because I don't miss mine."

"What time is yours?" I asked.

He replied, "Seven-thirty."

Coach Martin responded similarly. He told of rough times and difficulty and how coaching was not nearly as important as family. He wasn't concerned about wins and losses but the difference he could make in the lives of these men. Sports gods do not say these kinds of things, but followers of Christ do. Coach Cutcliffe and Coach Martin did, as Paul does in this text. They shirked fame and celebrity and talked about Jesus. Paul does the same in this text.

Why Do You Do This? (14:14-18)

Upset with the Lycaonians, Paul tore his garments, signaling to them that he was not a god but just a man. He was not merely interested in showing that he was "one of them" in a vain attempt to further bolster his reputation. Paul wanted to point them in a different direction. He called on them to repent of this lifestyle of worshiping the latest celebrity who came to their town. God is much different than the gods they were worshiping.

Paul had a simple sermon for them, a preview of what he says to the Athenians in Acts 17. The Lycaonians were to repent from this lifestyle and turn to the God of the universe who provided for them. There is no separate god of the weather, but one living creator of all things.

To paraphrase, we were created by the same God of Abraham, but often we are not worshiping the same God as other people in the world. Sometimes we're not even worshiping the same God as other Christians. All of us—pagans, Jewish people, and Christians—are prone to idolatry. We actually catch ourselves worshiping the idol of celebrity, fame, or fortune rather than God, who in Jesus Christ created the world. God provides for us, suffers for us, and calls us to endure persecution and be strengthened by God.

Sometimes I'm asked if we Christians worship the same God as Muslim and Jewish people. This is usually the wrong question to ask or even debate. The Bible itself testifies that there is only one God who created us all, calls every person good, and loves everyone. There really is no debate about that. We are either worshiping the one God, or we are idolizing something or someone else.

Instead, the Bible raises the same question that Paul asks: why are we worshiping the God we're worshiping? The only true and living God is the God of Abraham, Isaac, and Jacob, who reveals himself in Jesus Christ and offers a life that is modeled after Jesus. God creates all of us, but God does not seek popular celebrities, athletes, or politicians to make God more famous. More often than not, our lives get cluttered with the same gods of Muslims, Hindus, Americans, and everyone else. We prefer gods we can see and touch rather than the One who came as Jesus Christ, died for us, and rose again. That was not just a struggle for first-century Gentile people. Some of the Jewish people struggled too.

Attempted Stoning Confirms the Message (14:19-28)

Like Jesus' message in Luke 4, and Stephen's in Acts 8, Paul's message did not go over well. The response was only further confirmation that he was correct. With Gentiles still trying to offer sacrifices, some of the Jewish outsiders from the other towns came and tried to stir up the crowd. But do you know who struggled the most with this? It was some of the Lycaonian Jews. They are the ones who picked up stones to throw at Paul and Barnabas. Why? Because their god was contained in a book. Their god was not alive and with them. Just as Paul was not going to be idolized, he was also not going to be contained by the wishes of a group of people. Neither was Paul's God, the person of Jesus Christ.

Is our God the same God that Jewish people worship? We are created by the same God who called the Israelites and revealed God's self as Jesus Christ. But not all are worshiping the same God. In this case, these Jewish people are more interested in a stable Roman economy in Lystra than a living encounter with the Christ who calls them to suffer. They too want celebrities, success, and fame. If Paul and Barnabas are not going to provide it, then these people are threatened by it. How quickly things change for celebrities who don't follow the game plan. So if Jesus walked among us, and we deify him, what makes Jesus different from these others? Only Jesus rose from the dead never to die again.

The opposition attempts to stone Paul the way Stephen is stoned in Acts 8. Maybe Paul knew how to escape, or maybe this was all part of God's work. Like a superhero, Paul emerges victorious and moves onto Derbe. What is so amazing is that he and Barnabas backtracked through the places where people had attempted to stone them. They appointed leaders for the churches there, fasted, and prayed. And at the end of chapter 14 (v. 27), they were celebrating how God had opened a door of faith to the Gentiles.

Tearing Off the Clothes

So the real question is not, "Are we worshiping the same God?" According to Acts, if you are not worshiping Jesus Christ, you are not worshiping our

God. The question is, "Why do you worship Jesus, the resurrected Lord, the way you do?" It's pretty common for people to turn people into godlike characters. That's no surprise. But how do you respond when they do?

Paul sets us up for a confrontation with the powers—both those who think God is contained in a book and those who think that all the gods are basically the same. This is a totally different lifestyle than one built around Jesus as Lord.

Do you worship him as the crucified, risen Lord who invites you to repent and tear the clothes of those you worship, revealing that they and you are merely mortal humans? Or do you look around for the next person to follow to show you how to worship Jesus better? There's a big difference.

There's a great lesson to be learned for all of us. When celebrities and athletes look for fame, just point your friends to the One who took upon himself the form of a servant. Trust in God, and leave the hero worship to someone else.

Apparently, someone in Lystra listens to Paul and Barnabas. Ironically, it is someone whose mother was a Jew and father was a Greek, a good mix of both of the problems in this town. We will not meet him until Acts 16, but you will recognize him as Timothy.

NOTE

1. Charles H. Talbert, *Reading Acts: A Literary and Theological Commentary,* Reading the New Testament (New York: Crossroad, 1997), 135.

18

Word of Mouth

Acts 15:1–16:5

If I throw a ball to you, or even pretend to do so, you have to be ready, especially if you don't catch well. You don't want to drop it, but you also want to protect yourself from the flying object. In the ancient world, word of mouth was just as important as the printed page. It was more like a game of catch. In order to catch the ball, you've got to be ready, paying attention, watching, and so on. Even if you fail to make a clean catch, even if you juggle it, even if you drop it, you'll try. In the first-century Roman world, what was *said* about what was written was just as important as the writing itself. How people listened and responded was just as important as what was written on the page. Few people could read anyway. They trusted the messengers. Then, they trusted what the messengers said about what was written from the other party.

The early Christians picked up on this. To deal with conflict and disagreement, often the presenting issue was not the real issue. The printed page could be misunderstood, since most of them could not read. From long distances, they had to decide how to maintain fellowship with each other and adjust to what the Spirit was doing in their midst. How would the church work out its disagreements with each other in order to maintain fellowship, especially when the church was filled with unexpected converts? They anticipated that the group would change based on communication events. It wasn't merely that the text was written down and then read. The entire act of gaining the audience's attention, listening, testifying, and responding shaped the future of the church.

Acts 15 is a communication template for the church as the Jerusalem believers listened, performed, read, improvised, and delivered a decision. If we follow the process, we watch how their fellowship was shaped and changed by each other. When the Spirit converts new believers, the

Jerusalem church learns that the church must take the lead to welcome them, and fellowship them, into the community.

Communication and Miscommunication

Normally when we study this passage, we think of it as debate about whether or not to admit Gentiles, or about conflict in the church, or a combination of the above. But I'd like to study this as a communication template. The communication itself shapes the outcome; at least this is the way I believe Luke presents it. This passage gives us a window into the world of ancient listening, testimony, preaching, letter writing, communication, and how things can easily be miscommunicated. It's a sign of compromise among this first generation group of believers. But it also marks a transitional moment in the history of the church.

Remember also, this passage was read aloud to churches. So the way they processed conflict also became a template for how they addressed future conflicts. But what we'll discover is, by going through the process, they were strengthened and the church commissioned new missionaries for the sake of God's mission.

First, let's look at an overview of the chapter. In this passage you have a combination of several forms of communication and miscommunication. It's an early Christian *dia logos*, literally "from the word," as used in 15:27.

> Mission Team Faces an Issue (15:1-5)
> Debate (15:6-7)
> Peter's Testimony (15:7-11)
> Crowd's Response (15:12-13)
>   Silence
>   Listening
> James's Response (15:13-21)
>   Four Guidelines from Leviticus 17–18
> Four Witnesses Deliver the Message (15:22-29)
>   Letter
>   Word of Mouth (*dia logos*)
> Antioch's Response (15:30-33)
> New Team Commissioned (15:35–16:3)

Like an annual religious convention, the passage begins with a mission team and ends with the appointment of a completely new team. In between, some Jewish people from Judea present them with an issue that threatens to undermine their work. Jerusalem hosts a meeting, commonly called "the apostolic conference," to decide the issue. Really, it's a sort of symposium, a full-scale communication event with testimony, response, debate, response, and communication.

The Presenting Issue: Do Gentile Believers Have to Follow Jewish Law? (15:1-5)

When the Judeans arrive in 15:1, they claim that Gentile converts must be circumcised in order to become Christians. In other words, these leaders want to require adherence to Jewish law in order to be in fellowship with the church. It's a real challenge to what Paul and Barnabas have already experienced, that salvation comes by grace and is a gift of God. God has already done "signs and wonders" among the people (15:12). But the Judeans, probably Pharisaical believers, are very much entrenched in tradition, believing that "it is necessary to circumcise them and to order them to keep the law of Moses" (v. 5, ESV). Why is this an issue? There is more than one way to be a Jewish person in the ancient world, and certainly more than one way to be a Jewish Christian. They themselves are divided over what it meant to be Jewish. Scholars generally call this time in history "middle Judaism," a collection of various groups, six of which are listed in the Gospels and Acts: Pharisees, Sadducees, Essenes, Zealots, Herodians, and the Way. The question this text addresses is how the followers of the Way should incorporate Gentile believers into their community.

Testimony: Can Jewish Believers Fellowship with Gentile Believers? (15:6-11)

After a debate in Jerusalem, Peter rises to give his last speech in the book of Acts. It is his valedictory address, and we won't hear from him again. Peter reframes the issue: *It's not about whether Gentiles can be saved because they are saved by God. Why would we burden them any further because of our problems?* (15:10). By using "we," Peter takes the issue on himself. *If God is moving in the Gentiles' hearts and not making any distinction among them, then we Jews are the ones burdening them by requiring anything beyond grace.*

From Peter's perspective, based on his experiences of God's signs and wonders, the Gentiles are already believers. There is nothing we can do to stop that, nor should the Jewish believers want to. The Gentiles don't need to be circumcised to get in; they are already followers of the Way. Now that's an entirely different scenario than what the Judeans presented. They want Gentiles to be circumcised in order to become believers. Peter responds, "You're a bit late; they're already here."

Responses (15:12-21)

The first response comes from the crowd: attentive silence. That's important. One of the first responsibilities of an audience is to listen. Plutarch described this interaction like a game of catch. The audience member is a "fellow-worker" with the speaker.[1] In the New Testament, there are several examples of active listening, including watching the speaker, drawing near, fixing the speaker with one's gaze or attention, remaining silent, and filling gaps. What's the gap in the speech? It's Paul and Barnabas's perspective. We know they have a different take on the events. The details aren't recorded (15:12-13), but the audience works on this together.[2]

The second response comes from James, Jesus' brother. Remember that Herod had already martyred another James, John's brother. One who was skeptical of Jesus, his own brother, is now the ostensible leader of the Jerusalem church, sort of the flagship church of the Way.

Let's recap the who's who:

- Peter—leader of the disciples
- James—leader of the church
- Paul—apostle to the Gentiles

James's message is that God has "taken out of them a people for his name" (15:14) and he bases his argument on Scripture. Paul and Barnabas have seen from experience. Peter describes signs and wonders of the Spirit. Now Scripture confirms what the others are doing. This description is an important move rhetorically. No one person or thing made this decision; these three come together to help inform interpretation.

The people who are "taken out" (15:14) are Gentiles who dwell outside of Judea. In fact, the scriptural precedent for this can be found in a fulfilled prophecy from Amos 9 and Leviticus 17–18. Its laws and rules were for "resident aliens," Gentiles who live in the land of Judea,[3] but James says that the rules applying to foreigners in their territory are now going to apply to all people.

Still, these newly revised rules are not going to be written to get the Gentiles to conform to Judaism. These rules are going to be written so the Jewish converts can be in fellowship and community with the Gentiles. Verse 19 says, "We should not trouble those Gentiles who are turning to God…." In other words, this is not about getting them to change so that they can be like us. Rather, James is asking, what can we do to change so that we can be in fellowship with them? These rules and this entire meeting are about our ability to grow so that we can be a part of what God is doing. In Leviticus, the laws were written to maintain the purity of the Jewish people. Now, what rules do we need to let go of so we can be in fellowship with them?

That is another important rhetorical move. The Gentiles are already believers; they are already followers of the Way. We want to be in community with them, but we are Jewish and have dietary laws and restrictions that prevent us from doing so. That should tell us, of course, that a strong group of Christians wanted to maintain their Jewish heritage while also following Jesus. But they also wanted to be in fellowship with Gentiles. So they choose four rules out of Leviticus 17–18 to keep. There were actually ten rules total, so why did they choose four? We don't know, but I have a guess that I'll share with you later. They chose to honor these four rules by abstaining from the following:

1. Idolatry: eating meat offered to idols, usually sold at a public marketplace after it had been offered to idols
2. *Porneia*: there were three kinds of *porneia* / promiscuity
   i. Incest
   ii. Homosexual practices
   iii. Adultery
3. Strangled animals
4. Drinking blood

Thus far, notice the change. They have gone from ten rules to four through active listening, the testimony of Peter, and the scriptural basis of Jesus' brother James. Instead of placing the burden on the Gentiles, they've taken the responsibility of fellowship on themselves. God is doing the work of integrating them into one community. That we can't question. Now, let's figure out what we need to do for ourselves.

Before we continue, let's take a look at one example in today's world. In families whose children have gone through a divorce, churches are often called to help couples discern issues of divorce and remarriage. Even though Jesus allows for divorce in cases of marital unfaithfulness, abuse, or abandonment, many times Christians divorce for other reasons. Divorced or divorcing Christian parents want to remain in fellowship with their children, grandchildren, and new spouses. A church wants to minister to members who have been through this trauma as well. How does a community discern a proper pathway? Acts 15 suggests that Christians can discern together how to remain in fellowship with other believers who have sinned and how to restore them to community.

Delivering the Message

So how did the apostles deliver the message? It's one thing for a group of people in Jerusalem to arrive at a decision. It's another to communicate that decision to those who initiated the problem. The four laws require four witnesses: Paul, Barnabas, Judas Barsabbas, and Silas.

The group wrote a conventional letter, dictated to a scribe and designed to be read to recipients. Along with the letter itself are four messengers to interpret what is said in the letter. The messengers are just as important as the message and the medium. They have a certain set of qualifications. They have "risked their lives for the name of our Lord Jesus Christ" (15:26). Presumably none of us fall into this category. Their method of delivery is to read the letter and then deliver a dialogue. Notice verse 27: the message is delivered, "from the mouth," *dia logos*. The Greeks do not have a word for "memorize." This is the closest we get to it. The method is improvisational. You read what is said, and you express it in your own words. There was room for both interpretation and improvisation. Four witnesses accompany the four laws: Paul and Barnabas, along with Judas and Silas. They send a letter along with the important component of communication "from the mouth."

Reception

Antioch received the message and messengers, were glad of the answer and interpretation, and were strengthened. The message changed the recipients. It seems here that they were propped up by the report. Notice that they read it to the congregation in verse 31, then Judas and Silas provided the word of mouth exhortation that made the congregation rejoice. In the letter, the council acknowledges that the Judeans "have gone out from us, though with no instructions from us, have said things to disturb you and have unsettled your minds" (15:24). Now the disciples strengthen them with many words. It's all word of mouth. It's as much what is from their mouth as it is what's on the page.

Remember what Jesus said in Luke 21: "I will give you a mouth to speak, and don't worry beforehand what you are to say, the Holy Spirit will give you the words to say." Now they practice that very thing with fellow believers. It's what I think is probably a first-century version of improvisation. Part of public speaking was not just the ability to read word for word. The speaker was given the chance to improvise and put it into his or her own words. It was a combination of paraphrase, interpretation, and restatement. They stayed within the theme, but they put it in their own words. This is what Judas and Silas do for the church. This is what strengthens the church.

One of the things we do as Christians is create a space for word of mouth. It's a place where five things happen:

1. Testimony
2. Listening and silence
3. Filling in the gaps
4. Reflection on the written word
5. Improvisation and interpretation

This process, by the way, is what it will take to discover whom, and how, we have fellowship with. It's also whom and how we share hospitality with in the world. This plan, however, does not always resolve conflicts. But it does help us through the conflicts.

New Team Commissioned (15:35–16:5)

With the decision made, how is the process going to affect the composition of the group? Everyone is strengthened, but there is still disagreement within the group. They might have agreed with how the process was handled, but they did not like the outcome. Or maybe they realized that, this task done, they could go their separate ways. Silas and Judas left and Barnabas and Paul stayed behind a while longer…until Paul and Barnabas disagreed, in essence, over whether to give John Mark another chance. Verse 39 says, "The disagreement became so sharp that they parted company."

Unity is not the only sign of the Spirit's movement; unity can actually indicate a barrier to the Spirit's work. By splitting up, painful as it undoubtedly was, Paul and Barnabas were able to travel to more places than they would have together while also training new ministry partners.

Imagine hearing Acts read in a congregation. The listeners learned in Acts 7 that unity for unity's sake can result in a stoning. The mission is more important. Now, in Acts 16:1, Paul goes back to Lystra to recruit Timothy, someone who had initially been left behind. His father was a Greek, his mother was Jewish, and now his mentor has found a way to accommodate him in the mission. Timothy is ready to exemplify the new mission, and Paul circumcises him to demonstrate Timothy's commitment to the mission and willingness to compromise.

Lessons Learned

So let's review for a moment. The presenting issue was not the real issue. The issue for James was not whether these people had to be circumcised. They were already believers. Peter attested to the fact; Paul and Barnabas experienced it; the Bible said it was so. Why they begin the process is not the real issue at hand. The real issue is table fellowship as Jewish believers extended God's mission. Three confirmations come together to move the church through this stage of development: the experiences of Paul and Barnabas, the signs and wonders of Peter, and the scriptural foundation of James. By reflecting together and listening together, the *dia logos* changes the outcome of the events and the identity of the group.

What's fascinating to me is that the book of Acts is read all throughout the Mediterranean world. Today, it's even read in a completely different hemisphere. If you were watching and listening to how the council arrived at a decision over difficult issues with people in their community, what would you learn?

This requires a process of *dia logos*. What is Christian dialogue?

1. Testimony
2. Listening
3. Filling in the gaps
4. Scripture
5. Interpretation
6. Communication
7. Commission

The process might not result in unity, but it could result in strengthening the church and fulfilling God's mission.

NOTES

1. William D. Shiell, *Delivering from Memory: The Effect of Performance on the Early Christian Audience* (Eugene: Wipf and Stock, 2011), 24.

2. Kathy Reiko Maxwell, *Hearing Between the Lines: The Audience as Fellow-Worker in Luke-Acts and its Literary Millieu*, Library of New Testament Studies 425 (New York: T & T Clark, 2010), 57.

3. Leviticus 17–18 lists ten. Charles H. Talbert, *Reading Acts: A Literary and Theological Commentary*, Reading the New Testament (New York: Crossroad, 1997), 141.

19

Household Believers

Acts 16:6–40

Philippi was full of believers. Just ask them. For a Roman colony on the banks of the Gangites River, they had to be believers. The Greeks named this city after Philip, king of Macedonia and the father of Alexander the Great. When the Roman army was looking for a retirement center to reward their generals, colonels, centurions, and others, there was no finer place than the palaces of Philippi. They were believers. They believed in the power of the Roman army; they believed in the might of the state. They believed in what had gotten them there: a strong army, a good government, people who worked hard, a thriving slave trade to do the grunt work, and the wealth of its residents to make the place boom. Philippi was full of believers. So what happens when what you believe in is threatened by a power you have never seen or experienced before? Two people and their families and households converted. Just about everyone else panicked.

One of the characteristics of an ancient city is the business of fortune telling, and the business profited from human trafficking. We take it for granted today that we no longer have street-corner soothsaying, but we still spend a lot of time and money trying to control the future. We base our plans for retirement on financial planning and pay close to attention to the weather forecast to plan our week. We often say, "Based on what we know of the past and these calculations, this is what we think will work in the future." Everything about our attempts to control the future changes when Paul and Silas arrive.

God's Intervention (16:6-18)

When God prevents Paul from going into northern Turkey and Asia, Paul sees a vision of a man in Europe, in Macedonia. When Paul arrives and goes down to a place of prayer, instead of finding a man, Paul discovers a woman. Her name is Lydia and she is in charge of this place of prayer. She is one of two women in Acts who have a house church. The other is Mary, the mother of John Mark, mentioned in Acts 12. Most people think that Lydia is a person of some means: a dealer of purple cloth, and the color purple would have been certainly valuable based on the difficulty in producing the color.

After Lydia and her household convert to the Way, Paul returns to the same place of prayer, and a slave girl/fortuneteller meets them along the way. The text tells us she's possessed by a python spirit, also translated a "spirit of divination" (v. 16). We do not know many specifics; the point is that the python spirit sounds like a snake. So if we're going to read this text, we have to read it with a snakelike sound in our voices: *These men are s-s-s-slaves of the Most High God, who proclaim to you a way of s-s-s-salvation* (v. 17).

It is fascinating that Paul does not confront the demon for possessing this girl, or even deal with claims about God being one of many. He's just annoyed. The demon keeps doing this for many days (v. 18), and Paul and Silas probably say something along the lines of "This isn't the kind of marketing we want."

On the lips of the python, you can hear a nuance suggesting the direction of things in Philippi. As Kavin Rowe suggests, Paul and Silas are serving the Most High God.[1] The implication from the snake is that their God is one of many, and this God happens to be the best. In other words, salvation can come from all sorts of ways, and this is a way that could be very good for your life. Paul, however, reveals that there is only one God and only one way, and the Philippians' economic and political belief system violates the norms of the Lord Jesus Christ.

Annoyed by the python, Paul exorcises the demon. Doing so unmasks the hidden economic motive of the girl's owners. They, and the entire city, are exploiting this girl for their own good.

Philippian Reaction (16:19-24)

The crowd reacts swiftly. They pull out all the typical opposition that you would expect in a "civilized society." As verse 20 suggests, in dealing with threats to their system, the Roman people slander them. They lean on anti-Semitism, saying, "They're Jews." They lean on their comfort and sense of normalcy, accusing the apostles of inciting unrest: "They're causing the whole place to be turned into an uproar." They appeal to a sense of patriotic pride and a bit of xenophobia: "These customs are not lawful for us Romans."

Why? Because the only house the Philippians were supposed to be dependent on was the house of Rome. The people in Philippi, who had fought to defend the emperor, considered him the *pater familias*, the father or head of the family of the Roman empire.[2] And the home, the family, was the seedbed for the state. The home was expected to train up citizens, send them to school, and thus produce good, upstanding, honest citizens.

In an offhanded way, the early church indicates they are not interested in any of these issues that concern the state. By going to the place of prayer, they are saying, "We're not trying to get people elected into office, and we're not trying to run the chamber of commerce. We're working on converting households. We don't need publicity or annoying marketing. God does the work of conversion and revolutionizes life."

As an aside, the church does not prevent or discourage people from working. But, if the sole motive is profit, then there is going to be a problem. Lydia is a good example of someone who has her priorities straight. She is a good businesswoman. God does not need the business or nonprofit sector to accomplish God's purposes. In Philippi, God uses households to do the work God needs to do. When the apostles are punished for their actions, they find another household to demonstrate this power to the world. It just happens to be inside the jail.

God's Intervention (16:25-27)

The Philippians react with fear and panic. Arrested because their exorcism caused slave owners a financial setback, the apostles sing and celebrate their circumstances. That night there is an earthquake. We do not know if God directly caused the earthquake, but the event points to God's purposes for the Philippian jailer. The event directs people's attention toward God and another household convert.

Just as Lydia was a businesswoman tied to the Roman economy in Philippi, the jailer is tied directly to the state. His life is bound up with his job. Jailers were also notoriously corrupt people.

When the earthquake opens the prison doors, the jailer has a crisis of belief. The earthquake is going to cause him to lose his position, job, and even his life, because the prisoners will escape and he will be held responsible. When he's about to kill himself, Paul shouts in a loud voice—*not the voice of the snake*—"We are all here" (v. 28).

The jailer discovers that Paul and Silas are talking (and singing) about something more powerful than an earthquake. He asks, "What must I do to be saved?" Paul replies "Believe on the Lord Jesus Christ, and you will be saved, you and your household" (v. 31).

The statement is loaded theologically and politically. He is to believe in Jesus as Lord—not Caesar. Jesus is King and Christ. The belief is not based on evidence of what he can already see. For most people in the world, this is their definition of faith—seeing is believing. Even when they see something right in front of their eyes, they still do not believe it and are threatened by it.

For Christians, believing is "giving your heart" to Christ.[3] Believing is seeing. By choosing to believe and giving our hearts to Christ, we are able to see everything we need and are provided with a Presence to guide us. It was not that the jailer needed to believe in everything, all the gods. Just the one God. This kind of belief leaves room for doubt, sacredness, ambiguity, and even wonder. We kneel dependently (not confidently) in belief. We surrender. We come not knowing all the answers, but knowing our faith has been shaken. We come because our lives have been destroyed. Or what we believed in is not going to work any longer. Or the path we traveled just cannot play out. Or we found that what we believed in locked us away.

And through his gestures (including falling on his knees), the cry of desperation, and the cry of helplessness, he finds salvation.

Contrast this humility with the Philippian slave owners. They too are dependent on the economy and the state. When God's power confronts them, they arrest the bearers of good news. Motivated only by profit, when their hope of monetary gain is gone, they are ready to have Paul and Silas killed. By contrast, once his livelihood and standing have been preserved by the prisoners' actions during the earthquake, the jailer falls on his knees and asks, "What must I do to be saved?"

Marks of Household Believers

Alternating between God's intervention and human reaction, Philippi is changed, not through city hall or local businesses, but through households. Whether in Lydia's house or the warden's, the household is the location for God's change in this city. Acts indicates that, in Philippi, there are four characteristics of household faith: God's intervention, conversion, hospital-ity, and baptism.

First, God intervenes. God speaks through dreams to send Paul to Philippi, where God exorcises a demon from a slave and uses an earthquake to convert a jailer. This is not our work but God's work through us.

Second, recipients and their families convert on the basis of faith, not evidence. Two households are saved. Lydia is a God-fearer, and the jailer is a pagan. The only evidence they have comes through Paul and Silas's presence. Presumably, the other members of their households make this decision personally; the point of the passage is not the private prayer of the converted. The passage points to the significance of the leaders. A woman and a man had powerful influence over the Philippians, even more influ-ence than the *pater familias* of Philippi, the Roman emperor. The empire's grip over the people is dismantled one household at a time by people who convert on the basis of faith in the unseen God of the universe.

The leaders of the households are also gifted to lead the churches. Lydia, and by implication, the jailer lead house churches. In Acts 12, Mary set the precedent for leadership of her house church. Now these two follow suit because they are gifted to do so. Lydia is not appointed a leader because she is a woman. Nor is she denied leadership for that reason. She leads the church because she is gifted for leadership.

Household believers demonstrate their faith through hospitality and healing. Lydia and the jailer welcome guests in their home. Like the Samar-itan in Luke 11, the jailer bandages the missionaries' wounds and provides physical aid.

Paul baptizes the converts. The ritual confirms the change that has already occurred in the household and provides a way to celebrate it. At the end of Acts 16, he returns to the place of prayer, where these events started and where God confronted the forces of darkness in the city.

I am reminded of a similar experience at Philip Yancey's church in Chicago, a delightful mixture of races and economic groups. They sched-uled an all-night prayer vigil during a major crisis. Several people voiced concern.

"Is it safe, given our inner-city neighborhood? Should we hire guards or escorts for the parking lot? What if no one shows up?" At length, they discussed the practicality of the event before finally putting the night of prayer on the calendar. The poorest members of the congregation responded the most enthusiastically to the prayer vigil. Yancey writes, "I could not help wondering how many of their prayers had gone unanswered over the years—they lived in the projects, after all, amid crime, poverty, and suffering—yet still they showed a childlike trust in the power of prayer."

Thinking through the logistics, Yancey and his staff asked, "How long do you want to stay—an hour or two?'…'Oh, we'll stay all night,' they replied.

> One African-American woman in her nineties, who walked with a cane and could barely see, explained to a staff member why she wanted to spend the night sitting on the hard pews of a church in an unsafe neighborhood.
>
> "You see, they's lots of things we can't do in this church. We ain't so educated, and we ain't got as much energy as some of you younger folks. But we can pray. We got time, and we got faith. Some of us don't sleep much anyway. We can pray all night if needs be."[4]

When Paul arrives in Macedonia, the city believes in the power of the Roman colony. Beginning at the place of prayer, God intervenes one household at a time.

NOTES

1. Kavin Rowe, *World Upside Down: Reading Acts in the Graeco-Roman Age* (New York: Oxford University Press, 2009), 25.

2. Mikeal C. Parsons, *Acts*, Paideia Commentaries on the New Testament (Grand Rapids: Baker Academic, 2008), 234.

3. Kathleen Norris, *Amazing Grace* (New York: Riverhead Books, 1999), 62.

4. Philip Yancey, *Reaching for the Invisible God* (Grand Rapids: Zondervan, 2000), 39.

20

World Upside Down

Acts 17:1–15

According to tradition, when the British surrendered at Yorktown, their musicians played a song entitled "The World Turned Upside Down".

> If buttercups buzz'd after the bee
> If boats were on land, churches on sea
> If ponies rode men and if grass ate the cows
> And cats should be chased into holes by the mouse…
> If summer were spring
> And the other way 'round
> Then all the world would be upside down!

The legend of the poem certainly fits the theme of Acts. When you trace the early church's movement in the book, you discover something very powerful and compelling. The Christians created a different kind of culture.[1] These were righteous people living out a resurrection-empowered mission. They were not empowered to carry out a coup. They had no interest in the tactics or the structure of the state. From their vantage point, the world was upside down, with people fully focused on idolatry and violence. By lifting their hearts to Christ, they were able to focus heavenward.

From the locals' perspective, everything seemed to be moving the opposite direction. While the followers of the Way confessed, "the kingdom of this world has become the kingdom of this Christ" (Rev 11:15, NIV), the Thessalonians accused the Christians of treason and sedition. They felt the world had been turned upside down.

Collision Course of the Resurrection

Up to this point in Acts, we have learned that the resurrection is a ground-breaking, earth-shattering force because:

1. Jesus is now King
2. The King looks like a suffering Messiah who came back to life with weapons of words, service, love, and sacrifice

In Acts, we've seen evidence of this power in the followers of the Way (chapters 1-12) and five communities where the gospel has already spread. Evidence so far:

1. Antioch—a universal mission begins to Jews and Gentiles
2. Lycaonia—snake demons are excised; fortune tellers are disrupted
3. Pisidian Antioch—resurrection sends salvation to us; a Roman proconsul converts
4. Philippi—households become the primary location of conversion; earthquake and hospitality confirms the Spirit's movement.

In Thessalonica, as Kavin Rowe suggests, the message that "Jesus is King" clashes with the business practices. Along with Silas, Paul passes through Philippi, Amphipolis, and Appolonia along the Egnatian way. In Thessalonica, they go to the synagogue, the gathering place for debate, and proclaim their message that "Jesus is King."

Charles Talbert explains,

> Thessalonica was the chief city of the Roman province of Macedonia, the center of Roman administration. It's an independent Greek city-state. It was governed by a group of five or six *politarchs*, presided over by a chief *politarch*. They were responsible for the maintenance and order of the city, and this city had a synagogue. They could impose punishment here on non-Romans without bringing in the governor.[2]

After three weeks of teaching, debate has led to conversions, and the problems in the city begin. Debate would have been an important feature of the synagogue, but the local leaders did not like the resulting change. Verse 3 indicates the source of their conversion and conflict is the claim that Jesus is the Christ. This statement of faith is loaded political language in a town full of people who owe allegiance to Caesar.

Conversion and Reaction (17:4)

The extremely religious Greeks and some of the Jewish people are disturbed by these conversions. Other Jewish men and leading women are converted. The change upsets people, and their strategy is to attack the host of the Way in Thessalonica, a man named Jason. Luke reminds us that this is a much more widespread problem than simply an interreligious battle. There are instances in Acts of anti-Semitism and anti-monotheism. In this case, the Way is offending political partisanship. Thessalonica is actually outside of Roman rule; it is an independent Greek city-state, making its own local legislative decisions. The mob that gathers outside of Jason's house delivers a verdict. Paul and Silas are not present, and they drag Jason before the authorities or *politarchais*. They can impose punishment on non-Romans without bringing in the governor, and the Jewish opponents want to endear themselves to the Greeks. Playing on Greek sympathies, the Jewish people of Thessalonica want to rid their community of Paul and Silas.

Charges (17:5-7)

As Kavin Rowe suggests, let's look at the charges in reverse order:

1. They proclaim another king—it isn't just the king Jesus who is a rival to Caesar.

2. They act against the decrees of Caesar.

3. They disturb what we would call "the peace" or "public order."

The accusation against Jason and the other converts is the same one made against Paul in Acts 21:38. The word *stasis* is only used two times in the New Testament, and it is only found in the book of Acts. It's an act of revolution or rebellion where a seditious action leads to a revolt. It's not just disorientation but riotous upheaval—turning the world upside down.

If we closely examine these charges, it's obvious that they're false. Christians are already in Thessalonica—so Paul and Silas haven't turned the world upside down any more than it was before. Christians do not riot;

the town does. The other king was actually Caesar, not Jesus. The rioters, not the Christians, are turning the world upside down.

Why would the Thessalonians accuse Christians of sedition? To make it appear that the Christians are the ones revolting. Caesar and subsequently the Romans are rivals to Jesus. There is no other king. If anyone committed treason against the Lord, it was the *politarchs*.

As Kavin Rowe suggests, Luke makes the carefully nuanced point that those who were following Caesar were turning the world upside down. The Christians are right side up, or in this case turned around. The Christians in Jason's house are meeting, organizing, and doing their thing peacefully. The Jews and the Greeks attack them, not the other way around.

Paul and Silas Debate in Thessalonica (17:8-15)

The *politarchs* take a bond payment as security. If anything happens again, the Way is responsible. Jason will be held accountable, but the *politarchs* do not realize a new king, Jesus, is in charge. The riots, lootings, and protests do not stamp out the church, evidence of Christ's power and presence in their midst.

By remaining calm and continuing to practice their faith, the Christian witnesses expose the source of upheaval—anything and anyone that acts against Jesus Christ as Lord. We don't have to look too far for examples.

On April 27, 2011, a tornado destroyed a large section of Tuscaloosa, Alabama. People rushed in to help. People's lives were shattered, their worlds turned upside down, but the tornado also exposed how deeply divided the community already was. Ravaged by racism, poverty, and sin, Tuscaloosa was suddenly struggling to rebuild. The moment that landlords and others received money from FEMA to rebuild their homes and apartment complexes, many of the rental properties doubled in rent, ensuring than many of the poor who'd been displaced still had nowhere to go.

Imagine a city the size of Tuscaloosa, with a prominent state university, FEMA, and Housing and Urban Development (HUD) resources. They can win national titles in football, but people are standing around looking for places to live, with checks to pay reasonable rates, but they can't even find anywhere that will accept their check.

It's a world turned upside down. So the city turned to the church for support.

Calvary Baptist felt led to build sixty homes for people who wanted to pay rent, pay their bills, but didn't want to live in this dysfunctional, unjust, upside-down world. Together, the department of HUD, Calvary Baptist, and the city of Tuscaloosa have repaired or rebuilt eighty homes. Jeanette Barnes was the first recipient of a home. Recently, HUD recognized Calvary Baptist for leading the way in disaster relief. Even more significantly, they have found their mission among the residents of the community. A tornado devastated lives; but through the power of the resurrection, they have turned the world upside down.

Living Outwardly with Jesus

The resurrection offers us stability in a troubled world. With Jesus as our king, believers today have a chance to live outwardly for him. Even in an upside-down world, we can bear witness through peace, service, and truth. We may not worship in a house like Jason's, but we can rebuild homes like Jeanette's. By doing so, we are living with people who are on the bottom, because we are there too.

NOTES

1. Kavin Rowe, *World Upside Down: Reading Acts in the Graeco-Roman Age* (New York: Oxford University Press, 2009), 99–102.

2. Charles H. Talbert, *Reading Acts: A Literary and Theological Commentary*, Reading the New Testament (New York: Crossroad, 1997), 156.

21

Down the Road to Athens

Acts 17:16–34

Twenty years ago, Kelly and I honeymooned in Vermont. One evening, we walked around downtown Burlington near the University of Vermont. As we strolled, we observed what would be described as an average secular, political university town. Students were talking, eating, sharing, and getting nothing accomplished, which is pretty typical of all college campuses, now that I think about it. A southern pastor living underneath the buckle of the Bible belt and unfamiliar with any college towns might be tempted to look around self-righteously and say, "This is what atheism will do to you. No mention of God at all! They all must be so miserable." But Burlington, like every other college town, is quite religious. The religion just happens to be information—data, science, history, facts, figures, philosophies.

Luke describes the city of Athens this way in Acts 17. It is a place that values information and knowledge, which isn't a bad thing at all. But Athenians equated "teaching" (v. 19) with "divinities" (v. 18). For believers, the highest pursuit of all is God, who is love. Luke addresses his work to someone named "Theophilus," a lover of God. This is a love revealed in the resurrected Jesus Christ. In a city that assumes it has it all together in the learning department, God announces that Jesus has died and has come back to life. This news destabilizes a world of ideas, opens the possibility for life, and reveals someone who could not be found through science and philosophy alone.

The only place we know of where Paul visited but did not establish a church was Athens. This speech is also the only message delivered by a Roman citizen exclusively for a Gentile audience. The passage tells us a bit about the context and the people. In Athens, we do not have anti-Semitism or traditional Judaism to contend with. We have the age-old problem of pluralism. The people ask, "Do all roads lead to the same God? Is Christianity just one of several religions to choose from? If we are all worshiping something, don't all roads lead to the same place, and eventually it's going to work out?"

Paul's Two Sermons

Before we take a look at the sermon itself, we need to know a bit about Paul's two sermons, one for monotheists like the Jews and the other for pagans like the Athenians.[1]

A sermon for monotheists. This sermon went like this, "You're worshiping the true and living God, and that God is Jesus." Galatians 2:15-16 is a good example, "You are monotheists, and Jesus is the God you're worshiping, and we come to him by faith, not through works. The proof is that he came back to life, and you saw him right here among you."

Why two different sermons? Monotheists are very concerned about turning Jesus into an idol, or worshiping multiple gods, or thinking that God is not one (see the Shema in Deuteronomy 6:4). By the way, when you are talking to Muslims or Mormons, this is typically the direction the conversation turns. They want to know how to get the God they already worship to approve of them, and they assume that it comes from obedience to what people say about what the one God says. They have a hard time with grace, and admittedly so do we.

Paul talks about Jesus as the true God, saying, "Jesus is the God you're trying to worship, but there is nothing you can do to get him to like or approve of you. He already loves you." In Galatians, Paul explained to Jewish Christians that circumcision is not a means to grace.

A sermon for polytheists. The second sermon is for Gentile polytheists and other religiously secular people. Paul says in 1 Thessalonians 1:8-9,

> For not only has the word of the Lord sounded forth from you in Macedonia and Achaia, but your faith in God has gone forth everywhere, so that we need not say anything. For they themselves report concerning what a welcome we had among you, and how you *turned to God from idols* to serve a living and true God, and to wait for his Son from heaven, who he raised from the dead, Jesus who delivers us from the wrath to come.

To a monotheist, Jesus is the God you are seeking. You come to him by grace through faith. To a Gentile—or a Hindu or a Buddhist—Paul delivers a different sermon. Polytheists believe in lots of gods, idols, and pursuits. The first step for a polytheist is not simply to accept by faith. The first step is to turn away from their host of idols.

If you are already worshiping one God, then all you need to do is receive the gift. If you are worshiping many gods, you have to smash the idols and repent first.

Many intellectuals and average Americans think that church is a nice thing but they would not want to have anything to do with such a community. They are "spiritual but not religious." Usually they believe in the value of some sort of civil religion. This faith is inscribed on our coins, "In God we trust." Who is that God? Christians say, "Jesus", but others say, "Well, the words refer to the Christian God but it can mean whatever god you want it to mean." When we stop talking about coins, a modern polytheist intellectual may say, "Just fill in whatever god you want. As long as you're worshiping somebody, you're fine. It will all work out in the end."

A Sermon about God to the Athenians (17:22-31)

Paul addresses the Athenians as he had the Thessalonians. The Athenians enjoyed a good debate and desired more information, so they invited Paul to the Aeropagus, a marketplace where debate with pagans could be held (v. 22). Their polite request for more information seems to be a good sign (vv. 19-20). Like other messages to polytheists, Paul preaches a message of repentance (v. 30), encouraging them to turn from idols and to serve a living and true God in Jesus Christ. This is a short sermon in four movements.[2] Based on an analysis of the Greek use of the word "God," the sermon's central focus is the person of God. The sermon answers the question, "Who is this unknown God?"[3]

- Introduction (vv. 22-23)—Paul greets his audience and introduces his topic: the evidence of their ignorance of God in their worship practices.

- Thesis—what you worship as unknown is now known.[4] There are no more excuses for "we didn't know." God is known already.

• Proofs—Paul offers five proofs from natural theology that God is actually known and can be known by the Athenians.

Before we move on, let's unpack these five proofs.

1. God made everything. God is not a wizard behind a curtain. God has placed indicators in nature so that anyone can see evidence of God and believe.

2. Diverse nations came from one person (v. 26). When you see diversity, it is the sign of God's handiwork. Diversity is a finger pointing to God.

3. Seasons, boundaries, and time are evidence of God's existence (v. 26b).

4. God is the source of life. Using a reference from Greek literature (the philosopher Aratus), Paul says, "We too are [God's] offspring" (v. 28). Some of the Greeks understood that we came from the same God.

5. Even though you are worshiping dead things, God wants you to find God. God has somehow used all these pursuits in life to get the Athenian's attention. God can use anything, even idolatry, to get people to think about God. God is not far from us. God's on your heart, near your lips. It's a revealed word (Romans 10:9), but it's not a secret. You do not need an education to understand this. It is not like a diploma. No, this is something that God is going to give, and God is going to use your knowledge to help you realize that God was right beside you all the time.

God has decided to overlook our ignorance and wants us to find God. Stone, wood, and money are the dead things God created. The Athenians have worshiped, trusted, and depended on the things God made rather than the God who made them. If we continued today, we would add weapons, technology, progress, friends, relationships, and jobs.

Returning to our list, the final part of Paul's sermon to the Athenian polytheists is:

- Conclusion/Call to Action—Paul calls the Athenians to repent because the time of the end has arrived, and the resurrection confirms God's work.

  I. The world is coming to an end. The same God who made the seasons has set the appointed time.

  II. You must repent from these idols.

  III. God raised Jesus from the dead. The resurrection is the validation and assurance that these things will come to pass.

The Athenians' (and Our) Mixed Reactions (17:32-34)

With rhetorical skill, Paul uses concepts the Athenians can understand to point them to a God who wants to be found. He references a philosophical text familiar to the Athenians to help explain. Thus, he "baptized" a Greek concept into God's truth. Paul explains that we don't represent God. God has come in Jesus Christ. God is not a thing, a book, or an idea. God is a person.

God requires a decision of repentance because there are consequences. The world is coming to an end. God is the judge.

As we know, some Athenians believed and others did not (v. 34). No official church starts in Athens, and we realize that it takes more than good preaching for a person to convert.

Who converts more easily? The one who already believes in a single God, or the person who has a lot of gods on the roster, all of which they have to give up first? It takes more than clever illustrations, PowerPoint presentations, and cool music. Something has to happen to them in order for them to change. Just as God raised Jesus from the dead, God has to intervene in their lives. Jesus must reach down and raise them up.

How should we respond to these conversations? Most of us are around nonbelievers every day who have all kinds of competing priorities. For a time, they are sort of numb to what is going on in the world. Occasionally you get into a conversation about the ultimate things. Paul reminds us of what to say to the question that people raise: Aren't we all headed to the same place?

What do you say to a pluralist? How do I talk about this with someone who says, "All roads lead to the same place"? Our best approach is to witness to the breaking of Christ into the world. We can follow Paul's proofs as a basic outline for a conversation, which we share in the spirit of humility, gratitude, and love toward others:

1. God created all these things that we think are other gods and pursuits, but not all those pursuits lead back to God.

2. We share this universe. This not an "us versus you" conversation because there is one world, one universe, and one God, available to both of us. [5]

3. God has placed a lot of signs along the way to point people to God—namely, the seasons, the diversity of nations, and your very life. Just look at the differences between a Northwest Floridian and a South Beach Miamian. Despite living in the same state in the same country on the same continent, we are so different, and God created all of us. Our diversity reflects God's image. Not all religions are pointing to the one true God. As a friend of mine, Matt Cook, once said, "It's like trying to explain the difference between baseball and golf. We're talking about two different sports here, the only thing we have in common is a ball. We're playing by two sets of rules. There is nothing you can do on a golf course with a baseball bat that's legal. It's a totally different arena. The one thing we have in common is that God has created all of us, and we share God's creation."

All roads do not lead back to the one true God. In order to understand this, God has to do a work of grace, which God does through Jesus.

1. When Jesus came, he died and was resurrected. That validated his existence and set in motion the end of the world. We cannot understand this; God has to reveal it. We cannot know God through the seasons; those are the fingers pointing to God, but they are not God.

2. The only thing we can do is get ready for that end by repenting and changing. The one thing that most people who are searching for God want to see is whether or not it makes a difference in your life. Are you really different than everyone else who says they are worshiping God?

One of the most fascinating things about spending time doing mission work in former East Germany, Croatia, and later St. Petersburg, Russia, is that the East Germans and Croatians experienced dramatic growth in their churches after the fall of communism. The Croatian evangelicals were leaders in refugee relief for Serbians and later Syrians. In both East Germany and Croatia, I discovered that, behind the Iron Curtain of communism, God was alive and well. However, God was not alive and well in the ways we thought God was. There was a very vibrant, active faith among the house churches. They did not put up signs and reroof the church. They did ridiculous things like pray and study Scripture and host people in their homes. They partnered with other nations, working with anyone who needed Jesus. When you were able to get into these countries, Christ was alive and well. They had repented and changed so that when missionaries arrived after the Iron Curtain fell, we saw that we were the ones who needed to be evangelized.

Russia also had house churches and seminaries that were reborn after the fall of communism, but the response among the people has been relatively flat. I asked my friends in St. Petersburg why the church was not growing as fast as in Eastern Germany. They said, "Our biggest problem is all the Westerners that came over. Instead of turning to Jesus, we turned to you. We wanted the things you had, but we did not want the God who made the things and that you worship."

What about those of us in America today? Do we want God, or the things God has made? God calls all of us—especially those of us with things—to repent. When we do, that is what makes the church such a vibrant place to be.

NOTES

1. I'm grateful to Charles Talbert for this insight.

2. Most ancient speeches were designed to consist of five movements: *Exordium, Narratio,* Propositio, Probatio, Peroratio (Conclusion).

3. Mikeal C. Parsons, *Acts,* Paideia Commentaries on the New Testament (Grand Rapids: Baker Academic, 2008), 249. "God" is inflected four different ways in the sermon.

4. Also known as the "proposition."

5. This conversation usually happens when people suggest that religion causes violence.

22

A Church for the City

Acts 18:1–23

Corinth was a city colonized primarily by Romans, many of whom were freedmen. Corinth was the sports capital of the Greek world, holding the Greek version of the Super Bowl, a strange mix of gods, sports, entertainment, and economics that makes our obsession with winning seem almost like a hobby. It was a very religious city. The residents loved gods; no one was an atheist in Corinth. Rather, they just largely worshiped themselves and trusted in the emperor to provide, give, and share with them out of his beneficent heart.

The people who had the longest-lasting effect on Corinth, however, were not the politicians or athletes, but the refugees. When the emperor Claudius forced all Jewish people to leave Rome, wouldn't you know who arrived? Two migrants named Priscilla and Aquila. They met up with an apostle who was a Jewish convert named Paul. They were looking for two things: communication and community.

Not only could Paul debate the philosophers in Athens, he could also work with his hands as a day laborer. Paul was a tentmaker, an artisan, and a factory man. If you had hired Paul, he would have been the guy who fixed your roof or repaired your plumbing. If you had an outdoor amphitheater, he could have prepared the canvas cover.

Together, Paul, Priscilla, and Aquila communicated the gospel and formed a community in Corinth. They were especially passionate about their fellow Jewish people. Silas and Timothy arrived from Macedonia, and the five of them began to connect and pool their resources. They offered leadership to a burgeoning band of followers of the Way that needed their assistance, support, and encouragement.

Going Alone

As we have come to expect, not everyone wanted to follow Jesus. Some of the Jewish people in Corinth rejected Paul's message because Paul said that the king of all is Jesus—a strongly political, partisan message for that day. It's easy to see why he proclaimed this kind of message. Priscilla and Aquila could testify why you should distrust the emperor.

But Paul made a critical mistake, one that church leaders often make. Instead of leaning on the community around him, he decided to take matters into his own hands—literally. Out of anger, he tore his clothes and shook the dust off, leaving his Jewish people behind.

We're not exactly sure what motivated Paul to react this way. He had faced Jewish rejection before. We do know, however, that this response is most common when church leaders want to move things along more quickly than the Spirit is moving. Whether it comes to the church newsletter, a committee meeting, or community outreach, ministers are notorious for living by the motto "If you want something done right, you might as well do it yourself."

Paul turns away from this team, makes a rash decision, and decides to go down the street. He realizes when he arrives that God isn't finished with Judaism quite yet.

A Church for the City

Paul found a receptive audience in a house near the synagogue. Titius Justus embodied "a person of peace." He was not a believer yet, but he welcomed Paul, served Paul, and provided the kinds of qualities that would be needed for the gospel to take hold in Corinth.

Wouldn't you know that the first convert was one who had initially rejected Paul's message—Crispus, the ruler of the synagogue?

God's Vision for the City

With Paul restored to God's plan, the Lord spoke to Paul in a vision about the two things that he would need to work in Corinth. They were the same things that Priscilla and Aquila had found: communication and community. God said to Paul, "Do not be afraid, but speak and do not be silent; for I am with you, and no one will lay a hand on you to harm you, for there are many in this city who are my people" (vv. 9-10).

First, God replaces Paul's fears with God's presence. Instead of being afraid of his fellow Jewish leaders or the Gentiles, Paul is to act knowing that God's presence is with him and his team.

God speaks to Paul the way God spoke to Isaac in Genesis 26. When Isaac was stranded in the desert with no water for his flocks, God spoke to him in a dream vision, saying, "Do not be afraid; I am with you." After water flowed through the well, Isaac's enemies the Philistines came to him. They held a festival and made peace. God's presence gave Isaac the confidence to act hospitably toward the Philistines.

Then God instructed Paul to communicate: "speak and do not be silent" (v. 9). As churches and cities work together, God strengthens us through the way we listen, dialogue, learn, and grow with each other. Just as seminarians are taught communication skills in class, so these skills transfer to a church and a city that need the gospel.

Then God offered Paul community. Before Paul arrived, God already had people in that city who would be there for him. They preceded, and followed, Paul in ways that Paul could never have orchestrated. Paul could lean on them and learn from them. This group not only included leading women like Priscilla but also deacons like Phoebe, who lived down the road in Cenchrae.

Communication and Community

As churches today, we often discover the community around us in times of crisis. It was certainly that way for my friend Kyle Reese. Just before Christmas in 2007, the sanctuary of Hendricks Avenue Baptist Church burned. Amid the devastating loss and grief in this place, Kyle said that he relied on two things: communication and community. He learned to communicate constantly with his congregation about the plans to rebuild. He found community in the people of Jacksonville, who reached across lines of faith to embrace the church. People from the Doctor of Ministry cohort at Northern Seminary sent help and support, as did pastors from many other churches. These ministers formed a community of faith across the country for him and for Hendricks. Kyle has had a wonderful ministry at Hendricks Avenue because he didn't have to go alone. Before he arrived, and after the fire, he served a church for the city.

23

What You Don't Know Can Change You

Acts 18:24–19:10

When we first brought my son Parker home from the hospital, my wife Kelly and I decided to bathe him. As "good" parents, both of us wanted to share the experience. Neither one of us knew what to do, and we didn't trust the other one to know either. We placed Parker in the sink and opened the brochure the hospital gave us explaining how to bathe him. We realized very quickly that their procedure did not explain how to handle a flailing baby. After several minutes of frustration, we decided to give him a bath our way—not the way the brochure instructed us. When it's your first time doing anything, forget the instruction manual. Just get it done.

When we talk about our bath as Christians, we experience some similar feelings. We ask ourselves, "What is the point or purpose of our baptism?" Along the way, Paul discovers several men who have been baptized, just not in Jesus' name. The passage asks us in whose name are we baptized and why.

The Traveling Paul

In Acts 18:24–19:6, Paul relocates his ministry to Ephesus for two years and is joined by his Corinthian friends Priscilla and Aquila. (Priscilla is usually listed first, indicating she was the leader of the two. Sometimes she's listed by herself.) When they arrive in Ephesus, they encounter a wonder boy named Apollos and another group of believers who have the same condition. They are followers of John the Baptist but not followers of Jesus Christ.

We like to think of Jesus as the founder of Christianity and Paul as the first missionary. Long before Jesus' ministry, however, there was someone just as significant as Paul preparing the way: John the Baptist. The same guy who'd preached in the wilderness had influence that apparently stretched as far south as the banks of the Nile River, where disciples of the Baptist sprung up to prepare themselves for the coming of the Messiah.

They prepared through an old cleansing ritual that the Jewish people had modified and adapted over the centuries into a sort of a ritual bath. John the Baptist did not invent the formula. We Baptists—who aren't even connected to the guy whose name we share—did not originate dipping; this was a Jewish tradition passed down for centuries through a process associated with the twelve tribes. As John the Baptist's followers prepared for the moment the Messiah was to come, they engaged in a holy ritual cleansing.

In John's case, he took them down to a river, dipped them in the water, and they came out ready and prepared. It was so popular by this time that it had spread through the words of people like Apollos in Ephesus and twelve others. John the Baptist likely even baptized some of Jesus' disciples. Andrew and his brother Peter, and James and John the sons of Zebedee, were likely followers of John at one point (John 1:35-41).[1]

What's the difference between John's baptism and Jesus' baptism?

John's baptism is for repentance in anticipation of a coming Messiah. Baptism is a cleansing, to prepare a person for when the Messiah will wield a winnowing fork and fire (Luke 3:17).

Jesus' baptism is an act of obedient living with Jesus as Lord and a testimony of the commitment. Jesus is not turning away from something. He is crossing over into a new territory and beginning a new chapter. In Jesus' name, baptism is not repentance; baptism is a sign that the change has happened. Jesus' baptism is a testimony that Christ was doing what God the Father wanted him to do. Jesus' baptism says that your life has already changed. Jesus' baptism confirms the gift of the Holy Spirit. John's does not.

Furthermore, John's is a response to fear; Jesus' is in response to a calling. One is a sign of the end times; the other is a sign that the world has ended and new life has begun. One thinks about change; the other says God has already transformed me. One has nothing to do with the Holy Spirit; the other has everything to do with the Holy Spirit.

All of this serves as background to Paul's encounter with Apollos. John's baptism is the ritual cleansing of a wild man, and Apollos had popularized it.

The Alexandrian Apollos (18:24-25)

Alexandria was the crown jewel of Egypt and a prized possession of Julius Caesar and his cohorts. It was one of the wonders of the ancient world. Nestled on the banks of the Nile River on the coast of the Mediterranean Sea, the city thrived with commerce, industry, trade, and scholarship. As a port city, you could encounter the world—the good, the bad, and the ugly. As a center of scholarship, the Alexandrian Library rivaled any collection of ancient books. The Library of Congress would be the closest we have by comparison today. The Jewish philosopher Philo lived in Alexandria.

A city of such renown came with problems. Historians tell us that ethnic strife was commonplace. The various Roman ethnic groups rarely got along, especially with the Jewish people. During Paul's lifetime, a riot allegedly broke out in Alexandria as the Romans fought against the Jews. Religious groups sprang up, and the city became a hotbed for Christian evangelism.

Second only to Antioch, Alexandrian Christians rather quickly became a powerful force in the early church. They began out of a movement of Jewish believers under the guidance and tutelage of people like the great Egyptian Jewish philosopher Philo and many of his students. Perhaps one of his students was none other than a guy named Apollonius whom everyone called by his nickname "Apollos."

To understand Apollos's popularity, you might need to know something about his message. If you think John the Baptist was weird, Apollos was smooth. Apollos had a marketing strategy. He dropped the camel hair and put on the Greek rhetoric. Apollos not only preached about a bath, he took a bath. He was eloquent; he was out of the seminary. He had gone to school, which probably meant his family was of some good stock. (The only Egyptian families who could afford an education were wealthy.)

Apollos was schooled, lettered, and ready. With his Jewish background, armed with the dipping ritual of John the Baptist, and with some philosophy under his belt, he sold the fire insurance of the Jewish world. If he had authored books, they would have been bestsellers. If he had been in charge of capital campaigns, they would have all been successful. He preached sellout sermons. In fact, he was so good, this prize boy had emerged out of the Jewish quarters of Alexandria and arrived in Ephesus. On this Sunday morning in our text, there are only a few words to describe him: he was eloquent (we've said that), but the term could also be translated "boiling spirit" (v. 24). You did not need to wonder what Apollos's passions were.

If you needed to be fired up, he could fire you up. If you needed to have purpose, he could infuse you with purpose. And if you needed to have vision, he could give you vision.

I have been to enough end-times religious revivals to experience this kind of charisma. You leave feeling afraid and worried about the condition of the world, and you are willing to do whatever the preacher says to do. I remember attending a revival of a popular Southern Baptist evangelist who made a career out of questioning people's initial salvation and requiring people to be rebaptized, even those who had been immersed once before in a Baptist church. He bragged frequently about the numbers of deacons who went through the ritual again. His message was built on fear over the condition of the world, the impending judgment of Christians, and the need to be dipped in the blood of Jesus. Apollos would have been a willing convert to this kind of message. But it wasn't a message in Jesus' name.

Apollos was John the Baptist popularized—with emotion, intelligence, and delivery, but without dependence, obedience, and love. Apollos was about good works and taught about Jesus, but he preached from a position of fear. Jesus preached out of love and is coming again to redeem and to finish the work he's started. We look forward with hope rather than anger. As William Willimon says, "John the Baptist invited us to come, be washed, sign on with the kingdom. Jesus' invitation was even more radical. Come, wade into the sea, die, be drowned, and re-created, be those who break bread in the middle of the storm."[2]

Baptism in Jesus' name is an act of trusting your life to someone else. You cannot baptize with an instruction manual; you have to trust. You are reenacting what you have done with Christ. You've stopped lying, cheating, and stealing. You've done everything you knew to do and still you can't fix life. Instead, the only thing you can do is to throw your life 100% underwater with Jesus. Apollos had never experienced anything like that until he met Priscilla.

Priscilla Teaches Apollos (18:26-28)

Acts 19 tells us that Priscilla had the spiritual gift of teaching. She is mentioned first here in the text because she takes the lead in the teaching ministry. She explains to Apollos a missing piece of a very large puzzle that gives substance to his enthusiasm.

Apollos discovers new information that changes him. John's baptism symbolizes the preparation we make before we receive the Messiah. His baptism prepares him for an even greater gift that Jesus gave through his baptism—the gift that God is changing him and the world. Instead of a focus on the changes Apollos needed to make in his own life, God was changing him. Apollos is not cleaning himself up, God is cleansing him. God is already on a mission of fixing the world, symbolized through Jesus' baptism.

Imagine for a moment how that relates to our lives today. Everything in your life that we are doing here at church, all the rituals from Sunday school to worship to singing in the choir to going on a mission trip, is just preparation. Preparation is good. We need it. Sometimes you get excited and maybe even an adrenaline rush. If you go to camp over the summer, it fires you up and makes you want to come back with renewed vigor. All of it, Priscilla says, is preparation for one thing: entering the waters of baptism where we fully understand *that* God has changed us and *how* God has changed us.

We talk as Baptists about the personal decision to follow Christ. It's a very personal, intimate moment between you and the Lord. But we also know the phrase, "I'm making a personal decision to follow Christ," is not in the Bible. We're really deciding to follow the way of Christ or, as Priscilla explains to Apollos, "The Way of God" (v. 26). We're going all in.

Baptism is the public sharing of the private decision to follow. When we are baptized, we are literally placing our fate in the hands of another person. It is the original trust fall. If you have ever played that game, you know what I'm talking about. Baptism is an act of public humiliation where you allow someone else, who symbolizes Christ to you, to lower you backward, literally taking you under so that you can know that this is what it feels like to die in Christ. All the old stuff—your sin, yourself—is dead. Because you have so much trust, the baptizer both lowers and lifts you out of the water. Forever after you are totally dependent on God's ability to continue to change you.

By reenacting Jesus' baptism, something happens to you that helps you understand what God has done for you already. Nothing else compares to the experience. This is the difference between everything that you do to prepare to receive Christ and the reception of Christ into your life. Once you receive Christ, your story changes. Prior to Christ, our story was built around one thing—self. What can I do to improve this world? What can I do to build a career? Have a family? Do whatever it is I want to do? Most of the time those are good questions and you will just be good for goodness' sake (as Santa Claus wants us to). That is exactly what society needs us to be. But that is not what Jesus does.

We encounter a Christ who does not say, "fit me into your plans." Baptism shows us that we are totally subsumed or submerged into his plan. We fit Christ's work. Christ's first word to us is, "I'll take those plans; you're headed down the wrong path. You're not a good planner. I'm in charge. You had been going that way. Stop. You've got to get to know me and understand that everything is about denying yourself. It's not about enthusiasm, Apollos. It's not about sincerity. It's not about core beliefs or values. I'm the change you can believe in, and everything you're doing is wrong. Everything."

For enthusiasts like Apollos, that is a scary moment. But it was so significant that Jesus passed baptism along to us. We are still reenacting it as one of Christ's ordinances.

Ephesians Are Baptized in Jesus' Name (19:1-7)

The experience of baptism in Jesus' name, which is the same as the baptism of the Holy Spirit, was not limited to Apollos of course. There were Ephesians who were followers of the Baptist as well. The conversation with this Egyptian immigrant Apollos is so significant that even Paul himself comes down to Ephesus to finish the work that Priscilla started. Paul finds people in Ephesus who are rallying around the reconstitution of the twelve tribes of Israel. They're getting ready for the Messiah.

Paul explains that belief in Jesus is accompanied by a gift of the Holy Spirit. He raises a powerful question to the Ephesians, "What baptism did you receive?" Another way to paraphrase that question is, "What is the point of your baptism?"[3]

Baptism in Jesus' name is accompanied by the gift of the Holy Spirit in four places in Acts.

1. Peter's speech in 2:38

2. The Ethiopian eunuch in 8:14-16

3. Cornelius's baptism in 10:48

4. Baptism of twelve Ephesians in 19:1-7

Sometimes the confirmation of the Holy Spirit comes through laying on of hands; at other times, it is through the gift of tongues. In every case, when there is a baptism in Jesus' name, the Holy Spirit is present. Acts doesn't tell us what causes the Holy Spirit to come; Acts shows us that baptism simply affirms the presence of the Spirit already there. Our understanding of baptism as Baptists is patterned after Cornelius; he receives the gift of the Holy Spirit before baptism.

What's the Point of Your Baptism?

The question that we wrestle with today is the one asked of the Ephesians: what was the point of your baptism? Was your baptism to make you feel better, please your parents, join the church, escape from judgment? These are very real, very good motivations.

The point of your baptism is to give you a very visual, tangible picture that you hold the rest of your life. It is like the uniform you wear that says, "I am totally and completely submerged under the story of Christ's work in this world." It's confirmed because the Holy Spirit has taken my brokenness and given me something that is to be shared with the church and the world. We ask ourselves, "Where is God's work and where can I share this gift?" It is that simple, but it's also that radical.

Another way we might ask this question is, "What has your baptism done for you lately?" Baptism is only the beginning of the movement. Most of us had no idea what we were getting into when that preacher lowered us into the water in the Trinitarian name, but we do now. Like most things in life, if we had known then what we know now, we would have thought longer and harder. Thankfully we didn't know. Now we are here, so what is the point of your baptism today?

How has the totally submerged death changed the way you spend a couple of disposable hours at night with your kids? What do you talk about as you are sitting around the table?

You have been backing off at work now for a few months, not fully retired but getting there. Christ has been writing a story over your life and is about to write a new chapter coming up—how has that affected the way you look toward this time next year? Where will you live? What will you do?

You just declared a major last month. I know that it's recent, but now you're into it and that course that looked so easy has turned out to be so hard. How does the reality that old things are passed away and all things are becoming new—because you are a new creation in Christ—affect who you are? Did you pick that major because you can make a good living or so that you can do some good in the world?

It's now been six months since you have had an honest conversation with the person you supposedly love the most. It doesn't feel like love and, honestly, based on what everyone else is telling you, it would just make a lot of sense to get out of the marriage. Even your Christian friends have said it would probably be better to get out. How has your baptism shaped the way you see the habits of your heart, her heart, your life together? If you surrendered to being dunked, what would it take to surrender what you want to do and look to what God wants?

My guess is, if you think back to that day, or anticipate that day, your baptism was a special day. It might have even been a thin place for you, a place where, as the Celtic Christians said, heaven seems to touch the earth. But the unique thing about baptism is that the event is only the beginning of the powerful effect it has on us. As we reflect on our baptism, we grow in our understanding of it. As we remember it, baptism transforms us into new kinds of people. As we listen to the words again, "Jesus is Lord," we suddenly rediscover that "I am a new person, not because of what I have done, but because of what this Holy Spirit is doing through me and in spite of me."

Everything for Apollos was just fervent, enthusiastic preparation until he ran into Priscilla. Suddenly the one thing that he had wanted to change for so long changed him. We can know a lot about Christ, but once we begin to understand the point of our baptism and have wrestled with it, suddenly a new spirit comes alive again and the Holy Spirit gives us the blessing of the rebirth of life and the gifts of ministry. Baptism takes all that passion and energy and channels it into living the baptized life.

Now we know John the Baptist, and we know Paul, and we know Jesus, and we might know Apollos, but do we have any idea what our baptism has done for us lately? Because what we do not know just might change us again into the kind of people that Jesus wants us to be.

NOTES

1. Based on John 1, it's likely that Jesus himself recruited Peter, Andrew, James, and John away from John the Baptist.

2. William H. Willimon, *Peculiar Speech: Preaching to the Baptized* (Grand Rapids: Eerdmans, 1992), 66.

3. Martin M. Culy and Mikeal C. Parsons, *Acts: A Handbook on the Greek Text* (Waco: Baylor University Press, 2003), 360.

24

A Monotheistic Assembly

Acts 19:11–41

Every year in May, thirty thousand people would flock to Ephesus. They would fill the city and sell their wares and ply their trades. They would come to see the temple of Artemis, the seventh wonder of the ancient world, and the place was magnificent—about two-thirds the size of St. Peter's Basilica in Rome. To show that you had been there, tourists purchased a silver statuette of the goddess. Ephesus held a shrine to polytheism and celebrated the economic prosperity brought by the worship of one of their many gods.[1]

Intentional or not, the growth of the Christian assembly destabilized the economy as fewer people bought souvenirs and attended the religious festivals. Ephesus felt this more than perhaps any other city in the empire. In response, crowds rioted. To get a feel for this moment, let's take a look at the events that led up to the disturbance.

God's Miracles (19:11-20)

Our story begins with another example of Christians unmasking the forces of darkness. This time, they do so by turning these forces against themselves. Word spread rapidly through Ephesus that Paul was a healer. Paul, of course, was not the healer. Like Peter and John earlier in Acts, the Spirit provided the cure; Paul was God's agent. A simple chart comparing Paul's work with the local magicians illustrates the difference.

God healed people through aprons and handkerchiefs Paul has touched. The magicians focused the whole experience on the exorcist. God can use medication, websites, therapy, books, and more to heal people today. Many times a cure comes—at least temporarily. The difference between Christian healing and today's cures is who is glorified through the experience. God is the focus of all Christian work, and the results are not always measured in medical charts, book sales, and offering plates, though sometimes they are.

For example, read about the seven charlatans in Acts 19. Sceva's seven sons want to use the power that Paul has as a magical sideshow. In this exorcism, the high priest's kids tried to use the force of the phrase "in the name of Jesus" as a spell to benefit their work.

We see this kind of marketing especially with self-help preachers who use Jesus' name to advance their ministries. Contrasting apocalyptic preachers who forecast doom and gloom for personal ends, self-help preachers use Jesus' brand—and the adrenaline rush that goes with it—to benefit themselves and the local leaders. For instance, take this recent quote from Victoria Osteen, spouse of the prominent speaker Joel Osteen: "When you come to church, when you worship Him, you're not doing it for God really. You're doing it for yourself, because that's what makes God happy."[2]

We rightly criticize religious people who use Jesus' name to accomplish their own purposes. They encourage others to obey God because it is good for us and because it makes us happy to obey God. Everything leads back to us. Let's not fault Mrs. Osteen too much. She's basically paraphrasing the "pursuit of happiness" from the Declaration of Independence with religious overtones, and we Americans love our shows of patriotism.

Scripture testifies to a different pattern. God comes to us to accomplish what God wants, not the opposite way. The resurrection primarily occurs not for our benefit but for God's. God intervenes in the world because God wants to bring love, truth, justice, hope, and light to the people. God wants people to come after God, deny themselves, take up their cross, and follow God. God's not here for our happiness. God calls us to pursue God because God is God. This devotion affects every arena of life—especially the economy.

If we have been following the trajectory of Acts, we already know what it is like when God's power confronts the forces of darkness. Sergius Paulus experienced that first hand. This exorcism confronts the "power" of the Roman economy. Interestingly enough, even the demons in the man recognize this, saying, "Jesus I know, and Paul I know, but who are you?"

The demons do not recognize who the exorcists are. Remember that the demons do recognize who Jesus is. When they come out of their host, Satan divides himself (Luke 11:18).[3] Jesus uses the forces of darkness against themselves to cause division. Satan can no longer stand.

Acts 19 highlights the economic impact on Ephesus. People are amazed and in awe of what happens. These sons of Sceva, or perhaps other magicians in the city, decide to purge themselves of the incantation books (vv. 18-19).

Some people have used this passage as an excuse to burn books in the name of Jesus. In our context, that activity alone draws more attention to the burner rather than Jesus and usually does more to publicize whatever is being destroyed. The passage is not an example story for us to "go and do likewise." The event demonstrates the effect that Christ can have on a community. People read and purchase different things because they are now followers of Christ. The result is that evil is exposed, and Christians get a good laugh out of the experience by mocking their opponents. Satan is divided, spell books are burned, and God is praised. All of this, however, is just a prologue for the widespread impact of these decisions in the community.

Ephesians Disturb Their Peace (19:21-27)

Paul sent Timothy and Erastus to Macedonia in preparation for stop there on the way to Rome, but he chose to remain in Ephesus a while longer. The passage understates the effect of these decisions when "no little disturbance broke out concerning the Way" (v. 23).

If you do not think this was the case, look in Roman historical records. After a wave of trials against accused Christians, a Roman governor Pliny the Younger wrote a letter to Emperor Trajan, noting the revival of the economy and the local ritual worship of deities:

> There is no doubt that people have begun to throng to the temples which had been almost entirely deserted for a long time; the sacred rites which had been allowed to lapse are being performed again, and flesh of sacrificial victims is on sale everywhere, though up till recently scarcely anyone could be found to buy it.[4]

Pliny wrote while the Ephesian economy was recovering from a recession caused by Christians. In Acts 19, Demetrius offers a first-hand account of the experience. The person most disturbed in our text is this leader of local silversmiths. Think of him like the head of the local silver union. He calls a meeting of the group to see what they could do about these followers of the Way, whose influence is lessening the demand for the silver Artemis statues that were the union's staple product. The industry is down, tourism is down, and they are struggling. Notice how the economy plays such a role in their outlook. (vv. 24-27)

If you don't think your faith affects the economy, pay attention to what Christians purchase—or what they don't. We are blessed not to pay taxes as churches, and some Christians tithe to the Lord. We even buy and sell certain goods and services.

Christians don't measure the success of a country based solely on the unemployment index. Jobs aren't the only focus for believers because many jobs aren't reflective of the resurrection's power. Gambling, payday lending, pornography, and sex trafficking enslave people to the idols of wealth, power, greed, and lust. In the ancient world, the Christians didn't openly boycott these groups. Instead, they opposed evil indirectly, by working and living based on the power of the resurrection to sustain them.

Demetrius's speech reveals another level of evil at work behind the scenes in the silver trade. Goddess worship just maintains the status quo. The Ephesians refuse to see that their trade is a death march and that their loyalty to Artemis is actually killing them. Demetrius needs to stir up a crowd in order to restart their way of life.

Jewish People Attempt to Defend Christians (19:28-34)

When the Ephesian silver union tries to start a riot, the Jewish people in Ephesus defend the Christians. Polytheists try to spread violence and chaos, but the monotheists work together. Their motive is clarified by Alexander, when the crowd pushes this Jewish man forward to speak to the would-be rioters. He "motioned for silence and tried to make a defense before the people" (v. 33). The Greek text indicates that he gestured to make a defense. The nuance is important. The gesture for silence is different than the gesture for a defense. By motioning for a defense speech, Alexander indicates that he is taking the position of the followers of the Way.

The gesture for silence was likely an upraised pinky finger. The gesture to alert an audience prior to a speech was the index finger extended with the middle, fourth, and fifth fingers folded. The gesture introduced a defense speech by placing the middle finger against the thumb and extending the other three, moving the hand forward to the right or left.[5]

The crowd, however, does not care about listening to a defense speech. They continue to shout. The gesture suggests to us that Jewish people attempted to defend the work of the Christians against the polytheism of Ephesus. The problems of Ephesus aren't caused by worshiping the one true God. They are created by people worshiping false gods.

Assembly Dismissed (19:35-41)

The town clerk successfully quiets the crowd. The clerk refers to an Ephesian tradition that the gods had made the town the home of Artemis (v. 35). He encourages them to remain calm. They have witnessed the exorcism and the book burning. The only person starting the riot is Demetrius—one of their own Ephesians. The clerk quiets the crowd to prevent riots and preserve the *pax romana,* "Roman peace" or "law and order."

The final scene contrasts two kinds of assemblies in the ancient world: the rioting local Ephesian "assembly" and the *ekklesia,* or the church assembly. They gather to announce God's reign. Demetrius comes to stir the crowd. Christians assemble to worship God. The Ephesians, including the Jews and the clerk, try to keep the peace. The Christians worship the Prince of Peace, with their lips and in their lives and through their wallets.

Conclusion

Throughout his preaching, Paul has no idea the Ephesians will stop supporting the Artemis trade. But now every facet of their lives is changing. Without any intention on the part of the apostle, the preaching of the gospel destabilizes the economy. The local festivals end and people lose their jobs because the Christians practice a different lifestyle. They worship Jesus intentionally. They are in love with Christ and don't have time for the other parts of their culture.

Throughout this experience, the Christians remain calm. Paul is off to the side; the believers don't even let him appear in the theater. Instead, the crowds work themselves into a lather. The Christians are the calming presence, demonstrating a different Way. The Jewish locals rally to support and defend their fellow monotheists.

In the face of opposition and loyalty to the local economy, we offer a calming witness and presence. When faced with questions about our own loyalty, we say, "Jesus I know, and Paul I know, but what are these people up to?" We offer worship of the one true, living God who affects everything, even our wallets.

NOTES

1. Charles H. Talbert, *Reading Acts: A Literary and Theological Commentary,* Reading the New Testament (New York: Crossroad, 1997), 178.

2. Victoria Osteen, quoted in Ron Ribiat, "Quote of the Day: Pastor Victoria Osteen," *Religious News Service,* September 5, 2014 <http://www.religion news.com/2014/09/05/quote-day-pastor-victoria-osteen/> (accessed November 13, 2015).

3. See Luke 11:18.

4. Pliny the Younger, "Letter to Emperor Trajan," trans. Betty Radice, Loeb Classics Library 59 (Cambridge MA: Harvard University Press), 10.96.3.

5. See my discussion of these gestures in *Reading Acts: The Lector and the Early Christian Audience,* Biblical Interpretation (Boston: Brill Academic Publishers, 2004), 149. Also compare English versions of this passage, and note the different ways translators have tried to approach this passage.

25

The Lucky One

Acts 20:1-12

The book of Acts opens a window to let us peer into the beginnings of the church, when people fell asleep in church and fell out of windows, when worship was as much debate as it was agreement, and when there were conflicts, missteps, problems, and fun along the way. In so doing, people will wake up to say, "Yes, wherever I was, there was God in the midst of us." When the early churches worshiped, participants prepared for God to come to them, which was especially true for one lucky young man in Ephesus.

The last time Paul was in Troas, he barely stayed long enough to say goodbye. Troas was just a way station on his journey. This time, he spends seven days there. Acts treats this part of Paul's life as a farewell tour, the last lap for the missionary and a commencement ceremony for the churches. They have graduated from Paul's school. These are his final speeches to the graduates. This was not the last time they would hear from the apostle, but it would be the last time he'd speak to them personally.

For parents, high school graduation (or any other) is not usually our last chance to say what we need to say to our children. The day is just another passageway on the journey. But still, it's the last time we give them instructions before they move into the next chapter.

The church in Troas chooses a fascinating venue. It is an upstairs room reminiscent of the place where the disciples last gathered with Jesus. Sunday was the Lord's Day when they celebrated the resurrection. However, it was a normal workday for Romans, and Christians would have had to work. In the evening, however, they could serve meals and fellowship. By meeting at night, they worshiped the Risen One without losing their jobs.

However, by meeting upstairs at night, the followers of the Way were also risking their reputations. The early Christians were accused (among many other things) of drinking blood and sacrificing children. It was a way for some Jewish people and Romans to marginalize them. They were called atheists because they did not believe in all the gods of the Romans and were scapegoated accordingly. Because most of them worked on Sunday, the evening services allowed them to meet on the Lord's Day, but it only reinforced the rumor mill.[2]

We also see the first sign of a youth group. Just as there are three mothers in Acts, there are also three members of the Acts youth group: John Mark, Timothy, and "Lucky." In Acts 12, John Mark accepted a call to missions. In Acts 16, Paul picked Timothy in Ephesus. In Acts 20, we meet Eutychus, the luckiest young man alive, whose name means "Lucky." He had the one quality that everyone else in the room did not have, the good fortune of falling asleep when Paul was around, but we'll discuss that problem in a moment.

In the text, Paul decides to extend a twenty-minute goodbye into an all-night message. Keep in mind that ancient Near-Eastern people did not sit back and soak up a sermon. The word here, in fact, is not preaching at all; it's a dialogue and a debate. Paul discusses a topic, offers his opinion, and the people respond. They would have had something to say. We see this in the Berean congregation as well, and the same response will be expected in Troas. The reason the sermon took so long is because people engaged with Paul about it. Everyone would be prepared to come, remember, and participate in their formation.

Memory, testimony, character, and generosity formed the character of Christ-followers. Christians chose from the whole cultural menu of engagement during worship. People would shout yes or no, try to correct each other, and interrupt the speaker to ask questions.

In the middle of all this, "Lucky" is not so very lucky. The text is quite specific that he falls asleep, deeply. He falls out of the third-story window, likely the same height as a modern second-story window. Paul naturally goes down to check on him.

A casual observer of this nighttime incident would expect the crowd to react with a great deal of commotion. Remember that the church is already accused of child sacrifice; they already have a problem with people thinking they drink blood. Now they're killing off a member of their youth group—the only member of the youth group in Troas that we know about. Much like Elijah reviving the widow's son in 1 Kings 17, Paul falls on or bends over Eutychus and raises him to life.

Something's missing here. If everyone is so worried, where's the reaction? Where is the wonder? Where are the crowds spreading the news? In a miracle story, we expect some form of shock and awe. If one of our students passed out, we'd be grateful to get them back, right? Not Paul. He returns upstairs, eats, and finishes the message until dawn. And everyone is pleased.

There's obviously more to this story than a cute miracle to illustrate first-century Christian resuscitation. I would suggest to you that Mr. Lucky is more involved in the miracle than we realize. Eutychus is the patron saint of anyone who has fallen asleep in church, not because he is the punch line of a joke, but because he represents a problem the church faces in moral lenience. These are people who have fallen asleep at the switch of their souls.

Two Kinds of Sleep in Scripture

Do you remember how sleep works in the Bible? Sometimes sleep is a gift from God: a Sabbath rest, a chance to lie down and know that God is with you no matter what. There are plenty of examples, and we could cite some.

Rest—Sabbath (Genesis 1)

Elijah's rest (1 Kings 17)

Jesus as rest (Matthew 18)

This is a positive, life-giving rest that's part of the rhythm of relationship. God offers us this rest continually.

There is also a dark side of sleep. That sleep also seems to come over you when you are at your weakest point.

Moral Leniency—Samson (Judges 16)

Jonah (Jonah 1)

Eutychus (Acts 20)

They are asleep spiritually because of sloth and indolence. The psalmist calls it *shenah,* the noontime disease. Usually marked by boredom, a person has decided to disengage from God.[3]

Remember the story of Samson. He's a strong, bright, handsome young man. It's not just Delilah who gets to him by tempting his desires. But what else happens? He's warned not to be around her. He's warned to watch out. And of course, when he falls asleep, he loses his hair.

Jonah. What does he try to do when he boards a ship bound for Tarshish? The first thing he does is sleep. Sleep can be the way we avoid our problems with a spouse or a friend. It's a way of procrastinating.

Even the monks warn us of the problem mentioned in the Psalms; it is what the monks and Ecclesiastes call *acadeia*—sloth, a lack of attentiveness.

I would argue that Eutychus falls asleep, not because he is tired from the prom or the day's work, but because he's turned off his mental switch. He has chosen not to be engaged. He's the one who has said this is just for old people or children or women, and he has gone up to the top floor to prop himself up and ride out the lecture.

Eutychus has no idea how lucky he really was. He worships a God who came after him through Paul. The traveling missionary goes to Eutychus, falls on or bends over him, wakes him up in a nonchalant way, and gives him another chance.

Paul is simply repeating a pattern from the Hebrew Bible. After Sampson's hair is cut and his eyes are gouged out, he gets one more chance to come back to life and activity. No matter how far Jonah runs, the fish transports the prophet back to the people who needs God. So here in a service of worship, the Lord sends his own apostle to reflect God by giving Eutychus one more shot.

The most important work of all is to be engaged in worship. Worship engages us with the living God. We don't come to worship to get something out of it. We come to worship so that God might invade us and pull something out of us. We mentally make a choice to stay engaged in the process, allowing the Spirit to wake us up in the places where we have hit the snooze button. In worship, we practice the spiritual discipline of watchfulness. Paul decides that he is not going to let Eutychus simply fall asleep and miss out on an opportunity to encounter a living Lord.

Worship brings us back to life with Jesus through the power of the resurrection. We have the privilege of coming, not just to hear a message, but to prepare a response to the message. We might not have an ongoing debate, but we do have the dinner table afterward, as well as the questions and the emails we offer one another. Like the early church, we break bread, share meals, and seek out people like Eutychus. We ask ourselves, who are the spiritually inert people to whom God is sending us? To those who've just sort of drifted off the radar, or fallen through the cracks because of negligence or weakness. God sends us rushing down to say, "They were dead. But thanks be to God, they're lucky enough to be alive again."

We know them; they're just lucky to be here, but they haven't recognized that it's either luck or providence. We go and change our lives into the ministry of reconciliation. We decide they are just snoozing, as Paul does with Eutychus. This is not about sleeping in church or a miracle; this is about attentiveness to the nourishing word around you. It is good to know that, even in the first century, they are trying to keep people from being bored.

When William Willimon was a Methodist bishop in Alabama, he had been talking about baptism with Nathan, a twelve year old who requested to be baptized by immersion. When the bishop arrived, Nathan told him, "They tell me you've never done one of these before. I'd feel better if we could have a rehearsal." The small church had borrowed a baptistery and put it in fellowship hall. After the rehearsal, Willimon preached on baptism in worship. They marched out after the service, and the church gathered around the baptistery.

As they were getting ready, Nathan asked, "Could I say something to the people?" Receiving encouragement, he said, "When my parents got divorced, I just thought I had died. I thought my life was over. But then you stepped up and became the family that God wanted me to have. I want to thank you for the Boy Scout troop and the basketball team and all the Sunday school classes and all the people who tried to put up with me and teach me through the years. I wouldn't have known about Jesus if you hadn't told me. I'm here today because it's taken me twelve years to figure out that what seemed like a lot of nice, caring people—that was God. And God's gonna continue to work on me, and I'm going to make you proud. God used you to get to me."[3]

God used you to get to me. It takes a lot more than just plain luck, doesn't it?

NOTES

1. I prepared this sermon for High School Senior Recognition Sunday.

2. Charles H. Talbert, *Reading Acts: A Literary and Theological Commentary*, Reading the New Testament (New York: Crossroad, 1997), 184–85.

3. William H. Willimon, *Peculiar Speech: Preaching to the Baptized* (Grand Rapids: Eerdmans, 1992), 122.

26

Commended to the Word of Grace

Acts 20:13-38

They didn't want him to go. They knew all too well what Paul would face in Jerusalem. Going back to the place where his journey began, he would stand trial and give a testimony. The warp and woof of Acts is much like T.S. Eliot described in "Little Gidding." The journey is to come back home and find it all new again.

> With the drawing of this Love and the voice of this Calling
>
> We shall not cease from exploration
> And the end of all our exploring
> Will be to arrive where we started
> And know the place for the first time.
> Through the unknown, unremembered gate
> When the last of the earth left to discover
> Is that which was the beginning…

Before Paul left to go where he felt God was calling him, he had a few things to resolve with the Ephesian people. Like a shepherd entrusting his flock to another's care, Paul uses his farewell address to equip the elders and the people to be the sheep under the care of God and their elders. He commends to them, and us, God's word of grace (v. 32).

When I was at Baylor, Mikeal Parsons assigned this speech to me. This was the first speech in Acts that I had to study as a speech. The paper was terrible, but I also knew there was something embedded in these words that is real. Paul's comments are quite striking for someone saying goodbye. I imagine it's especially so to pastors who have bid farewell to multiple congregations. Barring sudden death, we go into most jobs or churches knowing that we'll one day say goodbye in a healthy way. Good endings make for glad beginnings and prepare the way for successors as well. These are more than rites of passage; they are also times to bring healing and closure and to equip people for the future. Ministerial departures, especially when handled incorrectly, leave open wounds for both pastors and congregations. Paul gives us a model of how to bring closure to any situation in healthy, helpful ways. He also shows us how to prepare people for what's ahead.

The Ephesians did everything they could to prevent Paul from leaving. For three years Paul was in and around Ephesus. So Paul begins, not with a set of propositions (here are the things you need to know) or beliefs to espouse, but with the relationship that they share. Their relationship is intimate and real, authentic and precious. It is both a defense and an encouragement to the elders, which says something to all of us about what it means to be in the work of ministry. All of us are ministers. That is what sets us apart as people—we are part of the flock as much as we lead the flock, even those of us who are overseers of that flock. He uses the same imagery that Luke uses to announce and herald Jesus' birth; the first earthly messengers were shepherds keeping watch over their flocks by night (Luke 2:8). Now Paul says to these shepherds, "I want you to keep watch over the flocks by keeping watch over yourselves."

Before the shepherds could tend to the sheep, they needed to tend to themselves. Ezekiel, a familiar figure from the Old Testament, experiences a similar call first hand. Before Ezekiel prophesied to others, God closed his mouth and prepared him through a series of nonverbal pantomimes or sign-acts. After months of lying on his side, God opened Ezekiel's mouth, and he delivered God's message to the elders. Shepherds prepare to guard the sheep by guarding themselves.

Rabbi Edwin Freedman suggests that the leader-shepherd is to act as virus protection for the flock. His life, character, and decisions affect the flock as a whole. As the shepherd goes, so do the sheep. The shepherd lays down his life for the sheep and pays attention to what he exposes himself to and what gets into his system. As you pay attention to your habits, character, and life, so you are working to develop an immune system for the flock of God, protecting it from viruses.

The Holy Spirit grants the elders to be overseers for each other. Their role functions in the way that bishops do in mainline denominations. Paul's instructions, however, transcend a position or office. Paul essentially says, "You know you are in the work of the ministry. You are the people" (v. 28).

In many Baptist churches, ministers are compensated to do the work of ministry. Paul flips the model for the Ephesians. Staff are called and paid to equip the people to do the work of the ministry and to keep watch over you as you do it—to guard and to protect and to guide the flock.[1]

Why? Because within the flock of God there are always dangers, there are always wolves, and there are always people lurking around. Now what could that be? Well, the tension for a moderate Baptist church always arises around what it means to maintain this discipline of being moderate. In the *New York Times* in 2012, and more recently in his latest book, columnist David Brooks suggests that moderates are often accused of being compromisers, a middle way between two extremes that meet in the "muddy middle." From the perspective of the Baptist moderate tradition, however, there is nothing muddy or watered down about moderates. Moderates have a deep sense of history and recognize that there are rarely "one size fits all" solutions, individual quests for greatness, or exuberant feelings that conquer all fears and problems. Brooks writes,

> Moderation is based on an awareness of the inevitability of conflict. If you think that the world can fit neatly together, then you don't need to be moderate. If you think all your personal qualities can be brought together into simple harmony, you don't need to hold back, you can just go whole hog for self-actualization and growth. If you think all moral values point in the same direction, or all political goals can be realized all at once by a straightforward march along one course, you don't need to be moderate either. You can just head in the direction of truth as quickly as possible. Moderation is based on the idea that things do not fit neatly together . . . . To live a coherent life, the moderate must first find a series of balances and proportions. The moderate knows there is no ultimate resolution to these tensions. Great matters cannot be settled by taking into account just one principle or one viewpoint. Governing is more like sailing in a storm: shift your weight one way when the boat tilts to starboard, shift your weight the other way when it tilts to port—adjust and adjust and adjust to circumstances to keep the semblance and equanimity of an even keel.[2]

As Paul found in Acts 20, sailing away from the Ephesian elders, the resurrection of Jesus destabilized their world. It shifted the powers that be, and the elders would need to find the appropriate ways through the storm as they guided their flock.

Similarly, moderate Baptists don't build churches based on what we can do in the middle. We base a church on a historical memory, not simply a democracy. In the 1600s, Baptists came together to live, here and now, as a community protecting the freedom of churches and individuals to interpret scripture and practice religion without the influence of the state. They found, of course, a world that didn't want life to be lived this way at all. Others preferred the comfort of religion established and supported by the state to preserve its way of life. Baptists instead cast a vision of freedom, not coercion. They lived as the kind of people who are "commended to God and to the word of grace," someone "bought with Christ's blood" (Acts 20:32; 20:28).

A moderate isn't ultimately committed to an abstract idea. Instead, she has a deep reverence for the way people live in her community and for the animating principle behind that way of life. In Baptist life, moderates revere the fact that we are a faith community dedicated to the Christian life—that is, committed to the idea that people should be given an opportunity to make that decision for themselves.

This animating principle doesn't mean that all Americans or Baptists think alike. It means that we have a tradition of conflict. Over the centuries, we have engaged in many long arguments around how to promote the Baptist vision—arguments between individuality and community, literalism and contextualism, inclusion or exclusion.

The moderate doesn't try to solve those arguments. There are no ultimate solutions. The moderate tries to preserve the tradition of conflict, keeping the opposing sides balanced. She understands that most public issues involve trade-offs. In most great arguments, there are two partially true points of view, which sit in tension. The moderate tries to maintain a rough proportion between them, to keep her faith in line with its historic trajectory.

The shepherd tries to make decisions and maintain the very presence of God by remaining calm despite tension. Notice what Paul says to those who are worried about him leaving, "Keep watch and stay alert. Watch yourself. That's what Eutychus needed to do, but he fell asleep and out the window. Shepherds stay alert and calm in making decisions."

We are trying to make the same decisions in our community. We are positioned to hold these values in tension so that our families can live in a place where they learn the Christian life together, where they show and demonstrate love to the homeless, where a person can go out on mission and serve.

That's why we have people who can guard the flock. As Baptists, we're all entitled to our opinions, but that doesn't mean we're entitled to share our opinion without correction. We listen and we learn from each other, and we come out into the light trusting that we are guarding what Christ has already done in caring for and nurturing and loving the flock of God, that we are protecting an already guaranteed inheritance.

So when in doubt, what should we do? We should work hard to help the weak. That's more than a philosophy; it's our lifestyle. We live to give ourselves away; we live to do as Jesus instructed, for it is more blessed to give than to receive. By giving and sharing and unleashing our life, we are able to sacrifice and share for one another, and life comes full circle.

When Paul was finished, he surrendered. People threw themselves at his feet just as the people of Jerusalem once laid their cloaks at his feet. But this time, they weren't angry, seeking revenge on a believer like Stephen. They were blessing a man who had trusted this flock to new leaders. The voice of love was calling again as Paul sailed for home to discover his old world with resurrection eyes. By caring for himself, Paul knew the flock of God would be guarded by elders who could moderate the new world that the resurrection unleashed. By so doing, they would experience God's word of grace together in Ephesus.

NOTES

1. This imagery carries over in his letter to the church at Ephesus in Ephesians 4.

2. David Brooks, *The Road to Character* (New York: Random House, 2015), Kindle edition.

Part Three

Challenge of the Gospel

Our series through Acts began a charter for a common way of living under the reign of the resurrected Christ. With the people formed, part 2 (chapters 13–20) addressed the changes that occurred in cities across the Mediterranean world. The Spirit sends the people to share the gospel with both Jews and Gentiles in light of the power of the resurrection. Paul concludes this section of missionary activity to the Mediterranean world by returning to Ephesus, blessing the leaders, and receiving a commission from the people.

Part 3 (chapters 21–28) responds to the challenge of the gospel. The gospel invites listeners to change and encounters several obstacles along the Way. In order to successfully accomplish the mission, listeners must be persuaded, but the gospel also must confront the various powers and forces of darkness, showing who the true King is. Most of this section centers on the speeches that Paul delivers and the subsequent reactions of his audiences. God uses these circumstances to deliver the message to the world. Paul is just one of a number of major and minor characters in God's plan. In the end, we discover, as the writer of Acts does, that the gospel moves unhindered throughout the world.

As you dive into part 3, I encourage you to read these speeches aloud. Invite your congregation, children, spouse, or friends to play the part of the audience in the story and invite them to reflect. Each speech addresses a different kind of listener, one who mirrors those we encounter today in government, religion, and the legal system. Such people challenge our faith.

The gospel, however, does not need to be defended. The gospel defends itself. The resurrection sends us to bear witness to kings, magistrates, religious leaders, and family members. We adapt our style to fit the listeners' needs and questions.

Here are some of the audience members we will encounter as we examine the challenges of and to the gospel:

- Agabus: a prophet
- Phillip's daughters: prophetesses
- Lysias: a Roman magistrate
- Tertullus: a lawyer
- Ananias: religious leader
- Paul's sister and nephew: family
- Festus and Felix: governors
- Agrippa: Roman king of Judea
- Bernice: family member of the officials
- Publius: public leader

27

Ambiguous Decision-Making

Acts 21:1-16

Suppose a person was about to make a decision of a lifetime. As a believer, she had followed the path taught to her. She prayed about the decision, searched the scriptures, sought the advice of trusted people, and interviewed for a new position. She received an offer to leave her current field and enter a new kind of occupation. Everything was right, except one thing. Two very trusted, respected people in her life had two different views on God's will. One said, "I've prayed about this, and I don't think this is a wise choice for you." The other said, "I think this is exactly what God wants you to do."

Life rarely offers clear, compelling directions. In some cases, as we discover today, believers can pray to the same God and appear to receive two different answers. God's will is not a road map, a sign, or even an emotional feeling. It is a journey based on the presence of the risen Christ in the believer's life. His presence can take us to places that we had not planned and give us options that appear to lead us in opposite directions. In reality, God forms our character through the decision-making process and corrects some of our misconceptions about discerning "God's will for your life."

Travel Decisions (21:1-6)

As Acts 21 opens, Paul has decided that God wants him to go to Jerusalem. He is sailing through his previous pastorates to bid farewell to some of the people he has touched along the journey. The believers, however, are praying to the same God and believe they are hearing the Spirit declare that Paul should not go to Jerusalem. In fact, he bows and kneels near a place where he once persecuted Christians (21:5).

To reinforce the decision, and heightening the tension of the experience, Paul hears another word from God. When Paul arrives in Cornelius's hometown of Caesarea, Paul stays with an evangelist named Philip and his daughters, who are prophetesses. Normally in a text like this, our attention would turn to the fulfillment of the prophecy from Joel 2:28 paraphrased in Acts 2:17: "Your sons and daughters shall prophesy." Philip's daughters are the fulfillment as well as the model for women preachers today. The emphasis in the text, however, is not on the words that come from their mouths. Instead, a different prophet, Agabus, prophesies to Paul and tells him not to go to Jerusalem. Agabus has a good track record and is the voice of experience. He was right once before about a famine (11:27-30). Pantomiming the arrest of Paul, Agabus performs what will happen to Paul through the Spirit. Paul, however, will not be persuaded.

This is beginning to sound like the old joke about the man stranded on his roof in the middle of a flood. A police officer, a boat, and a helicopter attempt to rescue the man. Each time, he replies, "God will save me." When he drowns, he asks God why the Lord didn't save him from the flood. God replies, "What do you think the police officer, boat, and helicopter were there for?"

We might speculate that Paul is being stubborn. It certainly would not be the first time that hardheadedness entered the equation of Christian living. Who's right and who's wrong? What if they are both right?

Through most of my Bible studies, I have thought of God's will as some sort of formula. Reduced to clichés, we can recall a time when someone has said something like one of these statements:

- God said it; I believe it; that settles it.
- Find out where God is going and go there.
- Go backward and look forward.
- Let go and let God.
- Pray, seek God, repeat, and wait for a feeling to know what to do.
- Surround yourself with good people who can discern.
- Listen to God's voice and follow God's direction.
- Ask what everyone else would do in a similar situation.

When we reduce God's plan to a bumper sticker, our answers are always either-or. God's will usually involves multiple decisions on the part of both God and the individual, each decision relating to many possible outcomes within the range of God's kingdom. Arguably, God adapts God's plan according to human frailty and failure. Just look at Paul's journey to get to this point in his ministry. But now look at today's passage. In what appears to be one of the clearest times where God speaks through the Spirit to the apostle, Paul and the people sense two different things. God's will clearly cannot be discerned by domesticating a story, reducing it to a few principles and formulas, and moving on with life.

God's will is full of tension and paradox. It is hard to separate the divine will from human interpretation, even among people moved by the Spirit. It's ambiguous, and there is always an element of mystery. As I mentioned in a previous sermon, one of my pastor friends, Dr. Brian Harbour once remarked that he was never quite sure if he was doing "what God wanted [him] to do," until he moved to a new church, settled into his new home, and then could look back and see God's plan. He had to be faithful and obedient along the way. Parker Palmer expresses a similar sentiment in his book, *Let Your Life Speak*: "Only when we see [the] 'way closing behind us' can we look forward to determine the next steps."[1] So what is this next step for Paul? If both answers conceivably could have been correct, then something else must be at work. Paul's farewell to his friends is a Gethsemane for him.

Paul's Gethsemane (21:14-16)

In the face of multiple options and differing opinions, Paul expresses a desire and determination to do what God wants, even if it means dying. He takes Jesus' prayer in Gethsemane to a higher plane. Not only "if it is possible, let this cup pass from me," (Matthew 26:39, ISV) but Paul says, "This is the cup." The people respond to Paul the way Jesus prayed to his father in Gethsemane: the Lord's will be done (Luke 22:42).

Paul shows us that there is always absence in the midst of goodness. Just as cups must have space for water, difficult decisions must have space in them. Paul surrenders himself to the will of God, who accepts many correct answers and involves humans in the discernment process. For Paul, the most important was not whether he would go to Jerusalem but whether the people could experience the agony of decision-making the way Jesus did in Gethsemane. Are they willing to surrender Paul to the Lord? He has supported them and they have supported him, too, even as the Spirit tells them that God could let the cup could pass from Paul.

They disagreed on the next step, but they resolved the tension through hospitality (v. 16). Peter had met Cornelius in Caesarea, one of the cities first changed by the gospel. Now disciples from Caesarea present the first challenge of the gospel. The gospel challenges us to follow the example of Christ in our Gethsemane: "not my will, but thine, be done" (Luke 22:42, KJV).

Decision-Making in Ambiguity

Paul shows us that life is so ambiguous, no formula will ever suffice to explain God's will. God can direct our path many different ways; God simply promises to direct our steps when we trust in God. Part of trust is to make a decision and continue to follow God as it leads us down the path. God has contingency plans for our contingencies.

This means that all the answers that follow Jesus are correct answers. We have to surrender our need to have one right answer and open ourselves to multiple possibilities in the will of God for what God wants us to do and what God wants our world to be. It is God who enjoys a sense of the random chance. No matter what happens, Paul demonstrates a readiness to serve. The church is involved in a decision-making process that involves suffering and difficulty. We surrender to the mysterious will of God. About the G.K. Chesterton quote, "Gratitude is happiness doubled by wonder," Ralph Wood writes, "The greatest test of happiness is gratitude no matter what happens."[2]

So often, Christians carry the regret of a past decision with them today as well as the paralyzing fear of decisions that will affect the future. Neither is healthy. By discerning the Spirit and suffering through the decisions and their outcome, we are fulfilling what Jesus and the church prayed, "Not my will but thine be done." And we finally receive clarity.

NOTES

1. Parker Palmer, *Let Your Life Speak: Listening for the Voice of Vocation* (San Francisco: Jossey-Bass, 2000), 54.

2. Ralph Wood, *Chesterton: The Nightmare Goodness of God* (Waco: Baylor University Press, 2011), 35.

28

Speaking Our Language

Acts 21:17–22:29

In Acts 9, we hear Luke's account of Saul's conversion on the road to Damascus. Now we hear Paul's first-hand account of his conversion at a Jewish hearing. Each time Paul shares a testimony, he varies it slightly, and so do we. We adapt our testimonies to our audiences and situations by finding commonalities with our listeners and emphasizing the points that will help them relate to our message. Through the power of testimony, we speak the language of the heart: our personal experience with Jesus and his people.

On the Steps of Jerusalem

Saul's birthplace was Tarsus, but his formal religious training began in Jerusalem. As a young Pharisee, he had presumably served on the staff of the Sanhedrin with one sentence in his job description: round up followers of Jesus and make them stop worshiping him. When Saul "saw the light," Jerusalem believers pointed him in the right direction. When he returned from the Arabian Desert, the Jerusalem Christians sent him out with Barnabas to share the good news with others.

Now, Paul has completed his last mission on behalf of the church. Based on his letters, he had received offerings of support for the believers who had sent him out. The old city of Jerusalem needed him now more than ever. He had traveled to various cities, including Corinth and Philippi, asking for monetary support for the Jerusalem Christians. And Paul was convinced that the Lord wanted him to deliver the money personally to the poor, including widows and orphans being housed in the old city.

Luke edits the story of Paul's testimony to show its effect on Paul's life. As he weaves his experiences into the story, his character grows. Testimony is not just telling your life history, and neither is it a conversation about "what God has done for my life." The early believers did not describe the time, date, and place where they saw the Lord. Testimony is an act of character formation, not about them, but about Jesus. As believers grew in their faith, they "gave testimony to the resurrection of the Lord Jesus" (4:26). Testimonies are discipleship and do five things:

1. Adapt to their audiences.
2. Focus on Jesus (as opposed to the speaker).
3. Change and highlight details.
4. Give firsthand accounts of experiences.
5. Defend the person and encourage them to continue the work.

Let's take a look at the three examples of Paul's testimony in Acts.[1]

Examples in Acts 9, 22, 26

	Acts 9: Conversion	Acts 22: Jerusalem	Acts 26: Agrippa
Speaker	Third person from Luke about Saul	First person Paul	First-person Paul
Language	Retold in Greek	Delivered in Aramaic	Delivered in Greek
Setting	On the way to Damascus	On the steps of Jerusalem temple	In the King's court
Audience	General	Jerusalemites and Romans	King Agrippa and his entourage
Geographic Location	Stephen from Cilicia (6:9)	Paul from Cilicia (21:39)	No mention of Cilicia
Reference to Christ	"I am Jesus"	"I am Jesus of Nazareth"	Jesus
Companions' Reactions	Men speechless, hear a voice	Men see the light but do not hear a voice	n/a
Physical Result	Saul cannot see	Saul cannot see becuase of the brightness of the light	n/a
Reference to Ananias	Vision of Ananias	Ananias	No Ananias
Timing	Occurs after Stephen's stoning	Concludes with struggle over the influence of Stephen	Concludes with appeal to Agrippa

Disarming the Tribune (21:37-40)

Now let's take a look specifically at this speech of Paul's.

His friends had warned him about this moment: "Paul, let someone else do it; you know you will get arrested. The people in the temple might have been your friends before, and you might have been on their staff, but that doesn't matter anymore. They'll accuse you of something, trump up charges against you, make you look bad. And worse, they'll make us all look bad." They were right, but Paul was more stubborn about his faith and desire to get the goods to the poor people who needed them than he was worried about any harm that might befall him. And it seemed that Paul was going to avoid trouble. He was going through the Jewish rituals of purification in the temple, a weeklong festival, but when the seventh day came, some Jewish people who had come to Jerusalem from Asia saw him and recognized him. They remembered the riots they had accused him of starting in Ephesus and other parts of Asia. The rest, as they say, is history. They beat him so badly that Lysias—a Roman tribune—and soldiers had to rescue him from their hands. The tribune had Paul arrested as a means of protection more than imprisonment.

With the fortitude of someone who had truly fallen in love with these people—despite how they treated him—Paul turned to them on the steps leading to the barracks and made one last speech to the people. He gave his testimony, telling them why he could endure certain suffering and shame at their hands: so that they would have the gospel and food and assistance. To address the crowd, he had to have the permission of the guard. Can you imagine the look on his face when Paul spoke Greek, the guard's language? And Paul had to be shocked to learn that he and his buddies were thought of as terrorists.

Apparently it was so shocking that, when he turned to the crowd, Paul switched from Greek to Hebrew, the street language of ordinary Jewish people and one that doesn't even exist today. Most English translations say that Paul gestured for the crowd to be quiet (21:40). The gesture likely consisted of the thumb, index, and middle fingers extended, with the fourth and fifth fingers folded against the palm.[2] The crowd saw the motion and began to be quiet, but quieted further when they heard him speak in their common language (22:2). His words startled them into listening. They spoke the same language.

It is one thing to go to a foreign country and share your faith, but your testimony is something that you share primarily with people who know you best, the people who knew you before you were a Christian or the people who you grew up with.

This Is Our Story (22:1-21)

Paul adapts his testimony and, by so doing, teaches himself and forms character. Why? Part of the training for early Christians included hearing others' testimonies and sharing their own stories. They learned from others and shared the message. According to Acts, Paul would have heard, and learned from, this kind of message via Stephen.[3]

At Stephen's stoning in Acts 7, Saul watched the martyr paraphrase the history of Israel and confront the Jewish leadership in Jerusalem. Stephen knelt, surrendered to the Lord, saw a vision, and died a martyr's death. In Acts 20, Paul had a similar experience with the Ephesian elders. He pleaded with them, knelt, and surrendered to them. Now, Paul pleads with the Jewish tribunal.

He establishes common ground with his people and begins his story in his hometown of Tarsus, the capital of Cilicia. He cites his pedigree under the authority of Gamaliel (v. 3). He admits his wrongdoing by confessing his persecution, and he discusses the turning point in his life when Jesus appeared to him on the road to Damascus (vv. 5-7). He notes Ananias's influence, another devout Jewish man who treated him as a "brother" (22:13). Paul concludes his testimony by remembering the significant influence Stephen had on his conversion. The Cilician Stephen still has an effect on fellow Cilician Paul.

Division Over Methods of Punishment (22:22-29)

Instead of laying their cloaks at Paul's feet, as they did at Stephen's stoning, the listeners tear their cloaks. The tribune, who had not paid attention to Paul's statement that he was a citizen of Cilicia, orders Paul taken into the barracks and flogged. The ruckus dies down and a centurion intervenes to prevent Paul's flogging. Paul is safe for now because the Jewish and Roman leadership are divided over their plans for him. The gospel, however, continues to challenge people through believers' testimonies.

Speaking Our Language Today

Throughout Acts, Paul speaks a language that transcends dialects, that is not taught in books or courses, but that can only be caught by observation and learned from the Lord—the language of love. You see it when people were literally falling at Paul's feet in Ephesus, begging him not to go. He still knew that he must go to the people of Jerusalem, not because he wanted to be a martyr or to draw attention to himself, but because he knew those people had not heard anyone speak to them in the language of love for a long time. You see it in how he deals with a guard who mistakes him for a terrorist. You hear it in his message to the council and to the Sanhedrin. The language of Paul, Jesus, and the church is love.

We speak a different language than society's words of violence and retribution. Sometimes, we speak differently than many of the other people in the room. We definitely act differently than most people around us. We can choose the speech and the verbiage of condemnation and criticism, of gossip and degradation, or we can choose to speak words that all people can understand—of encouragement and forgiveness, of obedience and instruction, of peace not swords, of building up not blaming and belittling. That is the language of love.

There is a time when God speaks to all of us. God speaks to you on your level, either through the words of a Sunday school teacher, a mother at the kitchen table, an uncle out on the back porch, or a preacher who seems to be talking directly to you. If God can find the words to say, don't you think God can give you those same words to speak to people around you in their language, in their way, in their time?

Sharing your testimony is an act of discipleship. Saul was a part of the audience in Stephen's stoning, and now he's the one sharing. Saul has learned from the person he persecuted. Now, he's sharing with people who also persecuted Stephen.

The focus is not on your life but on Jesus' work. By telling Jesus' story, your life is changed and so are those of the listeners. Paul grows in his faith as he shares the influence that Stephen has had on him. By sharing his story, Paul is engaged in training. We don't need to be on the steps of Jerusalem to be confronted, but when facing challenges at home, Paul gives us a few methods to follow.

First, share personally, not defensively. At no point does Paul attempt to incite a riot. The crowd is already divided among themselves.

Second, share your experience, not someone else's. Paul shares a personal word about his encounter with the Lord.

Third, mention the people who have influenced your walk. Paul alludes to Stephen and states Ananias's role. When speaking to folks at home, mention people they know who have influenced your decisions. Make references your audience will recognize.

Fourth, remember that Paul is comfortable enough with frailty to admit where he was wrong. All of us have blind spots that are revealed as we grow in Christ. In Paul's case, his blindness is physical but temporary and his wrongs are old but not insurmountable.

Fifth, discuss Jesus' message. Paul wants the focus to remain on Jesus and the resurrection.

Sixth, translate for today. Paul is mainly concerned about his audience, inviting them to respond immediately. He doesn't leave the issues in the past but invites a new response. Testimony should take place in the present tense. What is Jesus teaching you now, and why does it matter to the listener today?

Through Paul's powerful testimony, he shows us how to speak our language to people who share our background. The gospel challenges us to do just that.

NOTES

1. Adapted from Ben Witherington III, *The Acts of the Apostles: A Socio-Rhetorical Commentary* (Cambridge UK: Eerdmans, 1997).

2. William D. Shiell, *Reading Acts: The Lector and the Early Christian Audience*, Biblical Interpretation (Boston: Brill Academic Publishers, 2004), 151.

3. William D. Shiell, *Delivering from Memory: The Effect of Performance on the Early Christian Audience* (Eugene: Wipf and Stock, 2011), 63.

29

Staring and Standing By

Acts 22:30–23:35

There are many ways to look at people for long periods of time. From a stare to a glare, the eyes and face say a lot about a person's message. In this passage, we watch how Paul disarms a religious council with his eyes and a few quick-witted phrases.

The only group now standing in the way of Paul going to Rome is the Jewish religious council. The last person in Acts to appear before them was Peter, who escaped. When Jesus stood before them, he was crucified. Jesus and Peter were not Roman citizens, but Paul was. Paul could not be flogged or crucified, but he could be detained for some length of time and be prevented from appealing to Caesar, though it was his legal right. Paul's trial is bad publicity for religious Jewish people. Some council members and a Roman tribune named Lysias rescue God's plan from the council. Paul has already dealt with Lysias once, but he'll come back and serve as the unwitting hero of the story.

Sizing Up the Council (22:30–23:1)

Prior to his hearing, Paul looked intently at his opponents (23:1). Once in Luke and throughout the book of Acts, staring and gazing play significant roles. Stares are used to heal others, defend yourself, or communicate with the crowd.

Glares and Stares in Acts
Healing
- Peter and the lame man (Acts 3:4)
- Paul and the lame man (Acts 14:8-10)
- Paul and the exorcism of Bar-Jesus (Acts 13:9)

Defense
- Stephen and the Jerusalemites (Acts 6:15)
- Paul and the Sanhedrin (Acts 23:1)

Communication with God
- Disciples (Acts 1:10)
- Cornelius in terror (Acts 10:4)
- Peter and the vision (Acts 10:11)

Communication with Others
- Servant girl at Peter (Luke 22:56)
- Disciples into heaven (Acts 1:10)
- Peter at the lame man (Acts 3:4)
- The people at Peter and John (Acts 3:12)
- A religious council at Stephen's face (Acts 6:15)
- Stephen at the glory of God in heaven (Acts 7:55)
- Cornelius at God during prayer (Acts 10:4)
- Peter at the vision (Acts 11:6)
- Paul at Bar-Jesus (Acts 13:9)
- Paul at the lame man (Acts 14:9)

In most of these cases, people stare at someone else. In 23:1, Paul and the council stare at each other, functioning as mirrors. For those who are moved by Paul, they reflect on someone who was once one of them and could have easily been seated on this council had he not converted to the Way. For those opposed to Paul, they see themselves in his face and lash out. Paul's defense cuts to the heart of the Sanhedrin. As Charles Talbert notes, "These leaders have given other Jewish leadership located throughout the empire the motivation to continue their oppression of Messianists. Up to this point, Paul has eluded their beatings, stoning, and death. Two questions remain unanswered for Paul: (1) whether the Jewish leadership will allow him to exercise his civic right to appear before Roman magistrates, and (2) whether Paul can shift the terms of the debate from the charges brought against him to the issue of the resurrection of the dead."[1]

The man staring now speaks ironically to the high priest Ananias, testifying that he has a "clear conscience" before God. He knows that Ananias does not. As Josephus writes, Ananias had a terrible reputation:

But as for the high priest Ananias, he increased in glory every day, and this to a great degree, and had obtained the favor and esteem of the citizens in a signal manner; for he was a great hoarder up of money; he therefore cultivated the friendship of Albinus (the procurator after Festus), and of the high priest [Jesus], by making them presents; he also had servants who were very wicked, who joined themselves to the boldest sort of the people, and went to the thrashing-floors, and took away the tithes that belonged to the priests by violence, and did not refrain from beating such as would not give these tithes to them. So the other high priests acted in the like manner, as did those his servants, without any one being able to prohibit them; so that [some of the] priests, that of old were wont to be supported with those tithes, died for want of food.[2]

Knowing Your Opponents (23:2-10)

Paul's turn of phrase provokes Ananias to interrupt, ordering him to be struck (23:2). This is a complex scene and can be read in many different ways. Is Paul attacking the priest, or is something else at work?

In verse 3, Paul responds to Ananias with a harsh, angry statement, "God will strike you, you whitewashed wall!" He accuses Ananias of acting like the tombs that are washed annually in the area, which are still full of death.

In verse 4, the spectators have a question of their own. In verse 5, Paul saves face by saying he did not know who Ananias was. He backpedals, disarming the crowd, and cites scripture, saying, "I did not realize, brothers, that he was high priest; for it is written, 'You shall not speak evil of a leader of your people.'"

The crowd is already divided, and Paul picks up on their concerns. He notices that the Jewish leaders represent two parties of the Jews. In verse 6, he cunningly raises one of the deepest rifts in Jewish theology: "I am on trial concerning the hope of the resurrection of the dead!" In other words, Paul says, "The Sadducees are attempting to try a Pharisee."

Imagine, for a moment, that you are listening to this story. The audience knows that Ananias is hypocritical. Ananias should be the one on trial. Could Ananias sit as judge on behalf of Roman law without an appropriate charge being brought, especially given his history of issues with the Romans and the Jews?

Paul probably does recognize his garb as being that of the high priest. Paul could be attempting to follow the law when he claims that he does not know that Ananias was high priest; but again, nothing suggests that Paul was ignorant of the fact. It seems to me that Paul feigns ignorance and mocks the high priest at his own trial.

When he testifies to his citizenship, this son of Tarsus claims both worlds openly and publicly, not covering up his cooperation with Roman officials. Paul turns the tables by reminding them of something they already knew: Ananias is a hypocrite to sit as a judge in the first place.

The people are expecting for Ananias to judge him, but Paul digresses, disarming the council by dividing them over the resurrection.

The Lord is Standing Near (23:11)

With Paul's successful division of the house, Lysias intervenes and dismisses the council. Paul goes back to the barracks, but there he has another vision from the Lord. As in Corinth, God speaks to him in a vision, promising to stand by his apostle. In his testimony, Paul remembers that the disciple Ananias "stood by" him (22:13). A centurion and the high priest's officers stand by Paul in testimony (22:25) and strike him (23:2). But in the end, the Lord stands with him and foreshadows God's own presence.

Just because the Lord is nearby doesn't mean we're going to avoid trouble. Yet God's presence accompanies us through trouble and assists us along the way.

Paul's Nephew and Lysias Thwart a Conspiracy (23:12-35)

More than forty Jewish people, in league with the council, pledge to not eat or drink until Paul is dead. Much to our surprise, we learn that Paul has a sister and a nephew, and they are in Jerusalem. The nephew overhears the conspirators' plan to kill Paul, and a centurion ensures that the message is delivered (vv. 16-17). The very people who had tried to injure Paul, accuse him, and turn him over to the Jews are now rescuing him from his own people.

Lysias becomes God's agent, writing a letter to prop up his own issues and save face (23:23-35). The very tribune who had ordered Paul flogged and tried to use Paul to get a promotion becomes the hero of the story. God uses the Roman government to get "Operation Paul" underway. We'll learn later how the church and state function in God's plan in Acts 27. For now, we recognize that even someone who is the perceived opponent of believers can be God's instrument.

Reflecting on a Plan

As you study this passage, it is helpful to imagine watching it performed as a drama on stage. The characters stare at each other as you and I listen to them argue. What do you do when you're watching two people fuss? Imagine a courtroom scene where you're observing a defendant divide the jury. We're not learning what we would do if we are ever in those circumstances. It's highly unlikely we'd face a religious or civil trial because of our faith. We are allowing their lives to reflect our lives back to us. We're reflecting, gazing, and thinking through our spiritual issues of hypocrisy, fidelity, and courage in the face of opposition.

The scene is not designed to teach us how to defend ourselves against religious opposition. The gospel does not need to be defended. It defends itself. This scene functions as a mirror for the council to gaze into Paul's life and see the Lord. Even a tribune can become an agent of God's plan. We just have to trust the plan.

"Operation Paul," the successful transport of a prisoner who shares the gospel, has begun. The secret agent in the operation turns out to be the Roman's own tribune, Lysias. When God is nearby, anything can happen; but God's plan will succeed. Just take a good, long look in the mirror. The Lord is near you.

NOTES

1. Charles H. Talbert, *Reading Acts: A Literary and Theological Commentary*, Reading the New Testament (New York: Crossroad, 1997), 195. Also note William D. Shiell, *Reading Acts: The Lector and the Early Christian Audience*, Biblical Interpretation (Boston: Brill Academic Publishers, 2004).

2. Josephus, *Antiquities*, 20.9.2.

30

Delayed Opportunities

Acts 24

The gospel does not come with a stopwatch, a timeline, or a schedule. We often don't know if a conversation is going to be short or long. No matter the schedule, God's plan gives us a chance to back up, take stock, and evaluate why there are so many delays. If we're in the midst of a gospel challenge, however, we may also learn more about the opposition and some of their issues too.

Paul has now arrived safely in Caesarea and must appeal to a Roman procurator named Felix. This official functions like a county judge, usually appointed by the emperor as a reward for retiring Senators. Felix, however, is unique among his peers in that he is a freedman, a former slave. According to the Roman historian Tacitus and the Jewish historian Josephus, Felix is corrupt. He resorts to bribery and maintains law and order by instigating riots in order to make it look like one of his subjects had violated the law. He marries a Jewish woman named Drusilla who, at the time, is likely married to another man. She is the sister of King Agrippa II, whom we'll meet in Acts 26.

To get a sense of his corruption, listen to a couple of accounts from Tacitus and Josephus. According to Tacitus:

> Felix . . . stimulated disloyal acts; while he had, as a rival in the worst wickedness, Ventidius Cumanus, who held a part of the province, which was so divided that Galilea was governed by Cumanus, Samaria by Felix. The two peoples had long been at feud, and now less than ever restrained their enmity, from contempt of their rulers. And accordingly they plundered each other, letting loose bands of robbers, forming ambuscades, and occasionally fighting battles, and carrying the spoil and booty to the two procurators, who at first rejoiced at all this, but,

as the mischief grew, they interposed with an armed force, which was cut to pieces.[1]

Josephus writes:

> Felix took Eleazar the arch-robber, and many that were with him, alive, when they had ravaged the country for twenty years together, and sent them to Rome; but as to the number of the robbers whom he caused to be crucified, and of those who were caught among them, and whom he brought to punishment, they were a multitude not to be enumerated.[2]

The Romans were cruel and manipulative. It makes Paul's defense an even more remarkable feat and illustrates why the gospel challenges both the speaker and the listener.

Flattering Felix (24:1-9)

As Paul's trial begins, we're introduced to a rhetorician named Tertullus. This is the only time the term "attorney" is used in the New Testament. The use of this term reflects the foundation of this study. The New Testament, especially the book of Acts, is conversant with ancient forms of rhetoric, just as it is with philosophy, religion, politics, and ethics. Most of the time, the speakers and writers use these forms of persuasion to appeal to their listeners. At other times, they will invoke the forms to undermine them later. In other words, God didn't verbally dictate these words in Acts. Using their own time and place, these inspired writers used the categories, words, images, and rhetorical modes of their culture. They knew lawyers and *rhetors;* they had heard of Cicero, Quintilian, and Aristotle. The question is not whether they knew them but how they used their categories to advance the gospel.

In this case, Tertullus flatters Felix, saying, "Your Excellency, because of you we have *long enjoyed peace*" (v. 2, emphasis mine). Ironically, Felix only maintains peace by stirring up trouble. Tertullus's case rests on accusing Paul of the same crimes that Felix commits to maintain his grip on power. In verse 5 he says, "We have, in fact, found this man a pestilent fellow, an agitator among all the Jews through the world, and a ringleader of the sect of the Nazarenes." The carefully nuanced argument accuses Paul of sedition and disruption of the peace.[3] Paul uses the argument to expose the farce of

Felix (and the Romans) as they lose their grip on power in the area. Luke picks up on the strategy and exploits the opening.

Paul's Defense (24:10-21)

Felix motions to Paul to speak with a gesture acknowledging that he has permission to address the charges. Likely, this motion would have been a hand extended from an outstretched arm.[4] Paul introduces his speech by acknowledging Felix's length of service as a judge, but not his accomplishments. He acknowledges that he is guilty by association. He says, "I'm a Jew, and I was in Jerusalem." Because he claims to be one of them, he states that he was following their rituals. He concedes that he believes what they believe (vv. 14-16).

Then Paul calls them out. Tertullus doesn't have any concrete evidence of rioting. The only thing that he's on trial for is something the Jewish leadership can't agree upon. In other words, they have made Paul the scapegoat. He's on trial for something that has divided the Jewish leaders: the resurrection of the dead (v. 21).

Delay Tactics (24:22-27)

When he hears Paul deflect their criticism, placing the charges back into the accusers' hands, Felix engages in the age-old political strategy of delay. *Let's just drift along here and see what might happen. Let's have gridlock.* And he adjourns the hearing (v. 22). However, by refusing to decide, Felix has actually decided that the leadership does not have a case against Paul. He already knows about the Way and recognizes where this case is headed. Felix exposes his own insecurities—that despite his scare tactics, he's afraid of what might happen to him if the Jewish leadership or Paul cause trouble. He also realizes that his own questionable relationships are in play.

Felix cannot accuse Paul of sedition because he does just that on a regular basis. It would be the pot calling the kettle black. He's involved in a tawdry relationship with Agrippa II's sister Drusilla.

When Drusilla arrives, the discussion moves to the heart of Felix's problem. Felix and Drusilla are actually interested in what Paul has to say "concerning faith in Christ Jesus." They discuss what Paul says about resurrection. Felix wants to treat this as an intellectual discussion, but in verse 25, Paul reveals that this belief is more than simply a mental acknowledgment of an event or the miraculous faith step of a small group of people. The resurrection affects all of life.

There are three ethical implications to believing in the resurrection: justice, self-control, and response to the coming judgment. To believe in the resurrection means that one's mind, actions, and attitudes will be shaped by the event. This is not an idea for a page in a book. Neither is it solely a historical event for us to celebrate annually with new clothes and powerful music. There are implications for a person who follows the resurrection lifestyle.

1. Justice. We will live justly, as Micah 6:8 tells us to do. We will no longer seek out retribution; but instead, through God's mercy and forgiveness, we will bring justice to the oppressed. Reflecting the themes of Luke 4, we will set the captives free, bring recovery of sight to the blind, and proclaim the year of the Lord.

2. Self-control. We will behave differently, with restraint, because Jesus has changed lives. A new order has begun that changes how we manage our passions, affairs, decisions, and norms. We will live within the boundaries that God has set out because Jesus is King.

3. Coming judgment. The resurrection brings the future into the present. At present, we anticipate a coming judgment and know that God will make all things right in God's time in God's way.

Paul decides to hone in on the actual issues that Felix faces but cannot address without exposing his own sins. The longer Felix waits, the more corrupt he becomes. He wants Paul to bribe his way out of prison, but Paul just wants to advance the gospel. Paul is not there to bribe Felix; he's there to expose him. The longer you delay the gospel, the more it reveals about your life.

What Happens When "Nothing" Happens

Acts 24 represents another interlude in Paul's life. When nothing seems to be happening, Paul reveals something we have not heard before about Roman life, the resurrection, and the persuasiveness of the gospel.

The resurrection affects life in community. While Paul concedes a point and waits patiently, he keeps the focus on the resurrection. He shows us that injustice undermines justice. When the opponents are corrupt, the longer they wait, the harder it is for them to behave correctly. Give them time; they will sabotage themselves. Felix does, and even a sterile discussion about resurrection turns into a heart-felt plea for change.

Paul reveals that the gospel embraces the three ethics of resurrection. These conversations are important for Christians to have today. More than simply concepts, they change life for all eternity. We live with justice, self-control, and knowledge that a judgment is coming.

Life and the gospel usually happen while you're waiting for the next thing to happen—for your opponents as well as for yourself. Make the most of the opportunity to examine your conduct and grow in holiness.

NOTES

1. Tacitus, *Annals*, 12.54.

2. Josephus, *Wars*, 2.13.2.

3. Kavin Rowe, *World Upside Down: Reading Acts in the Graeco-Roman Age* (New York: Oxford University Press, 2009), 73.

4. William D. Shiell, *Reading Acts: The Lector and the Early Christian Audience*, Biblical Interpretation (Boston: Brill Academic Publishers, 2004).

31

Final Appeal
(to God's Work)

Acts 25

If an eighth grader studies hard for her biology test, answers all the questions correctly, and receives a 62 on her exam, more than likely, a parent would be inclined to request a meeting with the teacher. If the teacher denies the request to change the grade, the parent will most likely appeal to the principal. But if the parent automatically bypasses the principal and appeals directly to the school superintendent, we would think it odd and strange, especially since there is a high likelihood the grade would be corrected. What if, however, the parent just needed an excuse to meet with the superintendent? If the parent receives an audience, he might just use the test grade to underscore some deeper concerns.

Paul does precisely this in Acts. When he could have simply waited for the governor to make his decision, which would have likely led to his acquittal, Paul decides to bypass the governor, exercising his Roman citizenship to appeal to Caesar before they have even convicted him of a crime. The Romans stumble over themselves trying to explain what this is all about. The only one who seems to know what's really going on is Paul. He wants to testify to Caesar.

Change of Venue (25:1-5)

Paul was arrested on two kinds of charges, one Jewish, the other Roman. He allegedly sacrificed at the temple and incited a *stasis*, or insurrection. After his arrest, he remained in Caesarea long enough to write several of his epistles. Acts 25 reports that there's a new governor in town. This time, it's Festus. Festus went to Jerusalem to check on the headquarters of the

Jewish state and returned to Caesarea to check on things at the Roman headquarters.

Paul's Jewish accusers are still determined to get Paul to Jerusalem. They have filed a motion for a change of venue. We can assume that Paul would be ambushed on the way to Jerusalem and made an example of, treated the way Paul had once treated Stephen.

This kind of plot, however, could cause riots and trouble for Festus. Paul's sister and nephew are already aware of the conspiracy, and his nephew has already acted once to save Paul's life, but the apostle's motives are revealed when he files his own appeal.

Appeal to Caesar (25:6-11)

Festus sits on a judgment seat, or *bema,* for a pretrial hearing.[1] The Jewish leadership sends a small delegation without a lawyer like Tertullus (from chapter 24). This time, the accusers surround Paul in a circle the way the Sanhedrin did to Jesus.

Festus attempts to appeal to Paul's Jewish sensibilities and pass Paul off to the local people in Jerusalem, wanting the Jewish people to deal with their problems. Paul, however, reveals why he wants to appeal. To go to Jerusalem would effectively place the Jews on trial. He doesn't want to cause them any more trouble; these are his people, and they all worship God. He does not want to get involved in the tangled web of issues surrounding the temple's politics or create further problems by his presence.

Paul doesn't fear death. Even if he were to die while being transported to Jerusalem, he trusts in God. No, Paul wants to go to Rome so that he can announce to Caesar that he is not Lord. "Caesar is Lord" was inscribed on Roman currency. Paul wants to testify that the resurrection has changed the world (Acts 17:7) and that there has always been another Caesar in charge. That King is Jesus, and he is Lord.[2]

Deliberations with the Council (25:12)

In one brief phrase, Acts tells us that Festus has a decision to make. Roman citizens had the right to appeal their sentence to Caesar. However, historical records indicate that the local magistrates could deny their appeal. The local officials arbitrate which cases the emperor would hear. Festus has a responsibility to the empire and his position, and he is an instrument in God's plan.

This kind of passage usually gets swallowed by the conclusion that "Paul wanted to go to Rome, and so he made it." The story of Acts is not about Paul, however. This is the story of the gospel. God is spreading the good news throughout the world. Paul, Festus, the church, and everyone else involved are God's instruments. If Festus had denied the request, the gospel would have still spread to Rome.

Nevertheless, this story is another example in Acts of how God uses government. Unlike modern, secular democracies, which separate religious institutions from state agencies, Acts presents a society with complex relationships between religious practice and political life. Cornelius demonstrates that the state's work is commendable (Acts 10–11); the Philippian jailer converts (Acts 16); and Felix and Festus protect Paul (Acts 23–25). At the same time, Roman officials Lysias, Felix, Festus, and eventually Agrippa II are exceedingly corrupt. These people commit vile acts, and yet God uses them.

The apostles maintain one perspective whether the government and religious officials are good or bad: "We must obey God rather than men" (Acts 5:29). In Acts, sometimes the government is God's instrument and other times it's the world's obstacle. Religion does this too. In this case, God uses the state to accomplish God's larger purpose of spreading the gospel.[3] Luke is neither defending religious institutions nor defending civil ones. He's simply showing us that every human institution is subject to King Jesus and that God can use corrupt institutions to accomplish God's purpose.

At the same time, the political world works hard for its own preservation and power. They don't care one iota about Paul. The more Paul uses the state, the more the state self-sabotages. Even while using the state and religion, Peter says we ought to obey God (Acts 5:29). And, we remember from Thessalonica, Paul is preaching Jesus as King while the Romans are turning the world upside down (Acts 17:6).

Paul's main focus is not on who is the king. He could care less which governor or Caesar reigns. The important thing to Paul is carrying the message. He wants to ask, "Does the king surrender to the power of the resurrection?"

Resurrection has political implications, namely the ones we mentioned last week: justice, self-control, and the coming judgment. The king must recognize this power to surrender to Jesus as Lord.

So Festus deliberates and punts to Caesar, trying to keep the Israelites at bay. Festus avoids the problem of trying to convict Paul of something he

with which he is unfamiliar. Festus doesn't understand resurrection because he doesn't believe in Jesus.

Trying to Explain Jesus (25:13-21)

While Festus attempts to write the appeal to Caesar, Herod the Great's great-grandson Agrippa II arrives (v. 13). While Festus functions more like a local county commissioner, Agrippa II has a foot in both the Roman and Jewish worlds, a Jew who'd been appointed by the emperor. He's the fifth Herod in the Gospels and Acts. His half-sister and possible lover, Bernice, is the sister of Drusilla, Felix's wife. So let's just say there are lots of rumors about this family dynamic.

Paul has been summoned to a hearing about a miracle associated with his faith. Those who hold his life in their hands cannot even explain the nature of the charges. Festus acknowledges the "certain points about religion" (the Greek word can also be translated "superstition"; v. 19) and his ignorance, "I was at a loss how to explain . . . ." (v. 20). Verse 20 is bureaucratic speech for, "I have no idea how to explain this, but I'm going to let Caesar handle it."

Festus requests Agrippa's help in explaining to the emperor why this appeal is necessary. But ironically, Paul has convinced Festus, like Felix and Lysias, what is really at stake. It's Jesus, the same guy Agrippa II's grandfather, Herod Antipas, saw in Luke 23. Jesus is still around. This is the man who said in Luke 21:15 (paraphrased), "When you stand before kings, I'll give you a mouth and wisdom which none of your opponents can withstand or contradict." Paul has survived by keeping the focus on Jesus and the resurrection, and Agrippa II wants to see him personally.

Writer's Block (25:22-27)

For their interview of the lowly prisoner Paul, Agrippa II and Bernice enter as if attending a state dinner (v. 23). The scene highlights the foolishness of the Romans. They have a hearing so they can figure out what to write about something they can't explain. Festus attempts to save face in front of Agrippa II but admits, "I have nothing definite to write to our sovereign about him" (v. 26).[4] How does a person explain the power of God? A nonbeliever cannot explain that which he doesn't believe. Once you believe the resurrection, you realize you do not try to explain it; you testify to it. The Gospels and Acts are written by evangelists who record testimony. These books are not yet written, though, when Festus attempts to become one of the first people to describe what the resurrection is and why it matters.

Appeal to God's Work

In summary, we have learned several things about the steps the gospel has passed through in its journey out into the world. Paul appeals to Caesar because he wants to proclaim Jesus' resurrection to Rome. The Romans can't explain it because resurrection is unexplainable without Jesus. It's a miracle, one with world-altering repercussions. God uses the state as God's instrument to protect Paul while at the same time undermining the state. God exposes the farce of the government and its leaders' corruption while also allowing the state to protect the lead apostle. When Paul finally has the opportunity in Acts 26, he becomes the prosecutor and places King Agrippa II on trial. All along, Paul reveals what he's up to. He wants to share the message with everyone.

Remember the parent who appeals her daughter's test to the superintendent, but not because she merely wants to ensure a fair test grade. She has a message for the leadership. In the same way, Paul doesn't defend the gospel or become defensive. He speaks wherever he can. God opens the doors using a corrupt state. We, too, can be messengers wherever God sends us.

NOTES

1. There is no allusion here to the seat of judgment or mercy seat associated with the Ark of the Covenant, also known as the *bema*.

2. Kavin Rowe, *World Upside Down: Reading Acts in the Graeco-Roman Age* (New York: Oxford University Press, 2009), 96.

3. Mikeal C. Parsons, *Acts*, Paideia Commentaries on the New Testament (Grand Rapids: Baker Academic, 2008), 348–49.

4. The rhetorical term is *captatio benevolentiae*, often used to praise the worth of the listener and to endear the speaker to the listeners. In this case, it just shows how foolish the speaker and recipients really are.

32

On Trial with the Resurrection

Acts 26

Paramedic Jack Casey was called into the scene of an accident where a driver was pinned under a flipped car. Casey climbed into the vehicle, checked the victim's pulse, and said, "Don't worry. I'll be right here with you." As fuel leaked from the car, the other paramedics pried the man out using the jaws of life. Someone noticed that Casey could have easily left the car for his own safety. Instead, he risked his life to stay with this man. Someone asked Casey why he stayed. He replied that when he was a little boy, a dentist told him that he would have to anesthetize him to calm him down. He was afraid that he would never wake up. A nurse told him not to worry because she was going to stay right there no matter what happened. When he woke up, that nurse was sitting beside him holding his hand, just as she'd told him she would. For this paramedic, the childhood experience came alive at the scene of this accident so many years later. Casey looked back at a moment that changed his life, which influenced his behavior, and told a story about it.[1]

As Christians, we call this kind of story a testimony. We look back and see what happened that resulted in us becoming Christians. In the later chapter of Acts, Paul shares his testimony as part of his trial. In Acts 26, our passage for today, Paul uses his testimony to place the official on the defensive and prepare Agrippa II for his own trial with the resurrection.

Paul Versus Agrippa II in Caesarea

The last trial in Acts returns to the place where the Gentile mission began in Acts 11: Caesarea. Herod the Great built this town as a public works monument to his patron, Augustus Caesar. The city had a hippodrome, theater, bridge, and port to remind the people of the greatness of Caesar and to encourage their patriotic devotion. In this city, Peter had a vision that both Jews and Gentiles are invited into the kingdom of God and he met a centurion named Cornelius (Acts 10). The saga now comes full circle in Herod's prison, not with a dramatic rescue but with a trial. Agrippa II presides over the colony once ruled by his great-grandfather Herod the Great. Agrippa II and his half-sister Bernice are Jewish, and there are rumors of incest between them. She's been married multiple times and now arrives back in Caesarea for the pomp and circumstance of a Roman hearing. Agrippa's role is supposed to be simple: grant Paul's passage to Rome so he can appear before the emperor.

What appears to be a straightforward trial actually represents the collision between the Christians and the Herods. Paul and Agrippa II have been on parallel tracks throughout the book of Acts but here, at the end, they collide. One is in chains, and the other is on the throne. One is free, and the other is enslaved to his political authority.

On trial, Paul shares his testimony. To paraphrase, life for Paul is great for an obedient rabbi going to seminary, until Jesus caught up with him. Jesus changed Paul's life. He is first blinded, then is healed, then lowered over a Damascus wall in a basket under threat of persecution. Paul tells of more escapes and threats. Riots and unrest, even an earthquake, follow him. In fact, wherever Paul goes, the world seems to be turned upside down. Finally, Paul is so determined to go to Jerusalem that he ignores warnings that the journey will result in his arrest and death. Once arrested, he plays the final hand in his deck, appealing his not-yet-decided sentence to Caesar. As Paul explains to Festus, the resurrection not only brought Jesus back to life but rearranged the direction of Paul's life.

In the midst of the speech, the Roman attorney Festus interrupts Paul. I imagine this moment playing out like Jack Nicholson's famous scene from *A Few Good Men*, with Festus shouting, "You can't handle the truth." Governor Festus interrupts Paul and accuses him of *mania* (where we get the word "maniac"). But Paul uses Festus's interruption to reveal what's really happening. Paul is not the one on trial; Agrippa is.

In verses 26-27, Paul addresses the king, "Indeed the king knows about these things, and to him I speak freely; for I am certain that none of these things has escaped his notice, for this was not done in a corner. King Agrippa, do you believe the prophets? I know that you believe."

Agrippa attempts to divert Paul by implying that his prisoner is moving too fast. The king invokes the epithet "Christian," or "little Christs," used only once before in Acts. Agrippa says, "Are you so quickly persuading me to become a Christian?" (v. 28). Rhetorically, he concedes what Paul attempts to do, and Paul doesn't deny it. Instead of trying to defend himself against the charges, Paul uses this hearing to try to persuade King Agrippa of the truth of the gospel.

Paul replies that he hopes that the experience will do for Agrippa what Jesus did for Paul in Acts 9, "Whether quickly or not, I pray to God that not only you but also all who are listening to me today might become such as I am—except for these chains" (v. 29).

Agrippa II, who was summoned to grant the appeal to Rome, is now the one on trial. Ironically, this king says, "This man could have been set free if he had not appealed to the emperor." The reality for Paul is that the chains are signs of freedom. Paul, the jailed captive, is more liberated than Agrippa. The king is trapped by his power, his reputation, and his relationship with his half-sister. Paul holds the key to unlocking the door of the king's heart. The key is Jesus.

Testimonies of the Christians

Paul's experience in front of Agrippa II is one of three kinds of Christian testimonies in Acts. In the first, believers share about their experiences of the risen Christ in their homes and synagogues. The second is a *testimonia*—the Old Testament prophecies and paraphrases fulfilled in the lives of Jesus and his disciples.[2] The third proclaims how God had invaded their world and rearranged the courses of their lives.

At the 2012 Festival of Homiletics, I met a man named Danny from Danbury, Connecticut. He was attending for the first time so I offered him a ride to the meeting and asked him how long he had been a pastor. He informed me that he had been working on computers his entire career and planned to retire and become a woodworker, knowing that he could not make money working with wood. But he really enjoyed the hobby. However, on a recent trip to Israel, he was praying in the Garden of Gethsemane. In his words, his "calling was confirmed." He returned home, told his wife, quit his job, and went to seminary. This was his first preaching conference as a pastor.

Danny's life and Paul's experience offer similar testimonies. They were living a good, obedient life until the risen Christ caught up with them. In

Danny's case, he was a believer in a secular vocation, but God had another mission for him. For Paul, he was a believer in God who would now follow Jesus as the risen Lord.

Sometimes these encounters happen when life changes course, and we realize that the corrections are God's intervention. For outsiders like Festus, it seems ridiculous if not insane. We stand freely in front of people like them and engage in spiritual conversations.

Greg Hawkins and Cally Parkinson, in a recent study, revealed that Christians who have at least six conversations a year with people who are not believers are remarkably growing in Christ and becoming more like Christ. Verbally sharing Christ with someone is a catalytic moment. But that doesn't happen unless we believe that God is personally involved with us, sometimes in ways that we really don't recognize or believe are happening.[3] Personal involvement isn't usually described as an answer to prayer. That prayer is usually for something else. But instead, as we pray, we begin to experience a change of expectation, change of dreams and patterns, change of life and lifestyle in such a way that we become different.

When God intervenes, he becomes like the paramedic who rearranges his plans to stay with us in the midst of our lives. God whispers, "Don't worry. I will be with you no matter what happens." And suddenly, we have a story to tell to the nations.

NOTES

1. Robert Wuthnow, *Acts of Compassion: Caring for Others and Helping Ourselves* (Princeton NJ: Princeton University Press, 1991), 21.

2. The sermon on Acts 28 will discuss this kind of testimony.

3. Greg Hawkins and Cally Parkinson, *Move: What 1,000 Churches Reveal about Spiritual Growth* (Grand Rapids: Zondervan, 2011), 146.

33

The Perfect Storm

Acts 27:1–28:10

Sometimes in life, storms happen. They are not divine omens, punishments, or rewards. They are the results of life. We don't understand them, we can't predict them, but they do have important roles to play. When storms occur, they reveal the character of those caught up within and teach us about the culture of those around us.

The shipwreck in Acts is the "perfect storm," because it is neither divine punishment nor an omen. This kind of storm happens routinely during that time of year. God does not have to initiate a storm, as with Jonah, to work through events. In Acts, this storm reveals God's presence and Paul's character. The storm shows us how Paul behaves when he is away from the safe confines of home and when what has been carrying him is destroyed. If we want to see how Paul behaves in secret, this passage is our chance. And we discover that Paul is a man of character who is vindicated by God. Instead of trusting in the object that had carried him thus far or the people around him, Paul trusts in the God who speaks to him during the storm. God protects this innocent man from a viper's bite. Paul learns that he can trust God even when his expectations and security have crashed. Paul also learns that God is present in the midst of every storm, no matter what the cause.

Voyage To Rome (27:1-20)

Paul's voyage begins auspiciously. He's in the care of a kind centurion named Julius. As Mikeal Parsons notes, Julius offers us another opportunity to see Rome through its officials. Sometimes they are agents of God's will, and sometimes they are opponents. Often, they are both.[1] Depending on the individual, a person in government can advance or hinder God's plan.

In either case, God's plan always succeeds. Julius functions as an example of both, treating Paul respectfully and allowing Paul to say goodbye to friends but Julius does not listen to Paul's counsel about the journey. The more the centurion ignores Paul, the worse it gets.

By now, it's late in the sailing season on the Mediterranean. Paul advises them to stay on the island of Crete in a port called Fair Havens, but the centurion listens to the captain of the ship and the owner, both of whom are eager for the cargo to be delivered and purchased in Rome. They don't want to wait out the winter. Once the winds shift from the south, they sail. A Nor'easter blows them down the island. This weather pattern is the first sign that things are not going as planned. They fish ropes under the hull, knotting them to try to keep the boat together. After three nights, an angel of God speaks to Paul in a vision assuring him that he will stand trial. Comforted by the vision, Paul tries unsuccessfully to convince the men to eat, then to sacrifice their boat in order to save their lives. The people on board are about to learn what Paul already knows: we must often sacrifice the thing that supports us in order to survive.

Before we continue, think about the boat of your life for a moment. Everyone has their version of Paul's boat, and everyone sails on the seas of life. It's the institution or people who have carried you to this point on the journey. If you follow a traditional Baptist church upbringing, that's your family, your church, your school, your job, your home. Very few people follow that path consistently. Usually, we must deviate when one of these avenues comes under assault. The experience is not a warning or test from God, but instead an opportunity to trust God in the midst of life's many challenges. In Paul's case, this is what he finds in the middle of the Mediterranean Sea right before the end of sailing season in mid-October.[2]

Every one of us depends on an imperfect institution to carry us along in life. At some point, we learn to no longer depend solely on the boat. Instead, we grow in our character, take responsibility for our actions, and trust in a God who is present in the storm. Our faith must be formed and shaped in a character-building process most people call education and that you and I call discipleship. Paul's character is revealed on the island.

Paul's experience parallels another prophet who went through a time of undeserved suffering. The Old Testament figure Daniel does nothing to deserve punishment in a den of lions, and he is not magically vindicated because he conjured God to be on his side. However, God is always with Daniel. He is blameless and innocent in God's eyes. Daniel isn't delivered *because* he prayed three times daily. He isn't put into the lions' den to punish him because he *failed* to pray ten times daily. He is the victim of the way humans often treat other humans. Daniel is innocent. He believes in God. That is enough, and God delivers him. The process of deliverance reveals Daniel's character, faith, and the wonderful gift of grace that God gives. God even uses the hospitality of the unbelieving king Darius to save him.

Safely Ashore (27:27–28:10)

For fourteen days, Paul and the sailors travel through difficulty. The winds drive them across the Adriatic Sea and push them toward the island of Malta, just south of Sicily. After fourteen days, either because of seasickness or in an attempt to keep the ship heavy and thus easier to handle, they have not eaten. At daylight, they still can not see the land, but they see a bay with a beach. The boat runs aground on a reef, breaking the stern (27:41). As the boat breaks apart, the soldiers want to kill the prisoners so they won't escape, but the centurion wants to save Paul (27:43). He allows everyone to swim or float to shore. Once safely on dry land, more unusual things happen. The prisoners stay together and are greeted by welcoming islanders. While building the fire, Paul is bitten by a viper but doesn't die (28:4-6). The islanders think he is a god, and he's welcomed into a large palatial estate by Publius, the "first man" of the island. Paul heals his father, and many others from the island come to Paul and are healed (28:7-9).

If we automatically think of storms like these as some sort of divine test, we must ask what Paul needs to learn. If this is a punishment, as the islanders think, we wonder what Paul does to deserve such judgment (28:4). Yet when we acknowledge that storms come with life, we realize that these circumstances are part of the risk we take to breathe.

Three things converge to save Paul: his faith, his God, and the hospitality of the islanders. In contrast to the seafaring prophet Jonah, whose life and punishment are associated with a storm, Paul's experiences are much different. His faith in God and God's presence in the storm guide him through. When he arrives on the island, the residents show Paul and the others hospitality, even though they do not believe in God. They offer friendship, warmth, generosity, and education. The hospitality of the nonbeliever teaches Paul so much about God's presence. People that others perceive to be vipers are the ones with whom God is present.

Faith after the Boat is Lost

Our education and formation as Christians can prepare us for a new way to journey with God and can help us anticipate when plans will change, when our boats will be destroyed, and when we will be on our own. Our boats are not durable enough to withstand the storms forever, and when they fail, God will provide hospitality and philanthropy to remind us of God's presence in our lives. Then we will realize that, because we have been shaped and formed and educated in this value system we call "the Christian life," we will make it through.

In life, the only constant is the sea—ever-changing in every direction. Sometimes we are in the ocean, sometimes in Fair Havens, and sometimes it's too foggy to know the difference. For those who are believers like Paul, we learn that God's presence is constant. God neither prevents storms nor sends them, but he is present in those struggles. While we remain calm and wait for God's providential care and grace, something marvelous comes along: hospitality and philanthropy from strangers.

What we're asked to do is to provide the same to others. Like Paul gathering firewood and counseling his fellows to eat, our character and faith are educated by the storm. We learn from it and we learn from those who take care of us in our suffering. Sometimes it comes from the least likely nonbelievers, and we should reciprocate. God gives grace everywhere, even when we are isolated. When we are in the company of a few strangers, we understand that, despite their unbelief, they too can share God's love with us.

Let me give an example. A teenager named Ashley Reimer was fighting leukemia.[3] There is no amount of prayer, faithfulness, or church attendance that can ward off things like childhood cancer. It's undeserved, unjust, and flat wrong. Ashley had numerous bone marrow biopsies, nineteen spinal taps, an allergic reaction to a medication, a stomach infection, and a fungal infection.

In the midst of this, Army Colonel Ritza Reese realized that, because Ashley was undergoing chemotherapy treatments, there was a very good chance Ashley would miss her senior prom. So Col. Ritza thought, "Let's bring the prom to Ashley." She mentioned it to a nurse and a social worker, and from there the plans snowballed from what was originally going to be a little dance with CDs and snacks to a full-out formal party with a live DJ and catered food. They purchased formal gowns, and her friends came. A large, nice car greeted Ashley and her parents. A clown escorted them into the dance hall's foyer. Tables were covered with sapphire tablecloths, and a magician provided entertainment. Most importantly, they had a little normalcy during an otherwise difficult year.

I discovered through email that Ashley and her family were members of Rose Hill Baptist Church in Alexandria, Virginia. Even though this was not a feature of the original story I'd heard, the staff at the church encouraged me to share that part of their testimony.

A few weeks after I shared this story with my congregation in Knoxville, two guests arrived from Ashley's church. After watching the original sermon on the website, they wanted to come by our church and thank us for our prayers. They were en route to another event but made a point to stop in, share an update on Ashley's family, and encourage us.

I wish I could report that Ashley was cured of cancer. But a short while after these men visited, Ashley died. She died and awoke in the arms of her savior. Her testimony is still teaching others about the power of God's presence from strangers in the midst of suffering.

Ashley said in the article, "You realize who your real friends are. I've grown away from some friends and others have stuck by."

When life seems to be destroyed, that's when our faith, God's presence, and a few strangers guide us home.

NOTES

1. Mikeal C. Parsons, *Acts*, Paideia Commentaries on the New Testament (Grand Rapids: Baker Academic, 2008), 347.

2. Luke's view of the boat is much different than Matthew's. In Matthew 14, for instance, the disciples learn to stay in the boat with Jesus rather than get out of it. The boat represents the church and the need to row together to stay on course. In Acts, I think the boat is simply the many things that carry us along—family, friends, church—until we experience a crash. We often learn character through those experiences.

3. Mary Brophy Marcus, "For One Cancer Patient, It Was a Prom Night To Remember," *USA Today*, February 22, 2010, <http://usatoday30. usatoday.com/news/health/2010-02-22-ashleyprom22_cv_N.htm> (accessed September 9, 2016).

34

Life as a Tenant:
The Unhindered Gospel

Acts 28:10–31

How do you finish a story? "They lived happily ever after"? "They rode into the sunset"? "That's all, folks"?

Most stories end in one of three ways:

1. They summarize the story.
2. They describe what ultimately happens to the characters.
3. They are left open ended.

Acts ends with an adverb, so to speak. In other words, Acts ends with a blank. We don't know what happens to the main characters because, presumably, it hadn't happened yet. There was still more story to be written.

Send the Light

In Acts 1:8, Jesus sends his disciples to be witnesses to "the ends of the earth." Since people thought the world was flat, from Luke's perspective, Jerusalem is the center and Rome is the end. As the apostles move out, the missionaries realize the gospel arrives ahead of them. They form a common way (chapters 1–12) and see change in the cities (Acts 13–18). The old hymn "Send the Light" reflects one part of this theme: God sends the light, and the apostles track it.

> There's a call coming ringing o'er the restless wave . . .
> There are souls to rescue, there are souls to save!
> Send the light . . .

Let it shine from shore to shore . . .
Let it shine forevermore."

They also face the challenge of the gospel (Acts 21–28). Paul challenges people, and the gospel encounters rejection. Paul doesn't always arrive to receptive hearts. There are riots, difficulties, and disturbances. Problems, as well as opportunities, lie ahead of Paul. We should never tell a story about a door of faith opening without a story about a door of faith closing. But in Acts 28, despite these difficulties, God accomplishes God's purposes and trains those sending the light.

Rent Space for the Gospel (28:17-22)

The church in Acts begins in an upstairs room and ends in a house. We start with people praying together and conclude with an itinerant preacher proclaiming the gospel.

Like these characters in Acts, our role mirrors theirs. We begin as witnesses and end as tenants, renting space so we can share the gospel. As much as we are privileged to live in a land of private property, the gospel challenges us not to see ourselves as owners but as tenants. We have been given a responsibility to live as renters with an open-door policy.

In verse 17, Paul sits in his temporary house, calling together the local Jewish leaders. Normally, a handful of such leaders conspire against Paul wherever he preaches. Now a group of Jewish leaders are open to hearing Paul speak. Now Paul shows them hospitality, and they're ready to meet. As we've seen at each step, Paul wants to convert his people. He has no reason to stir up a riot; he invites them into conversation to talk about the "hope of Israel" (v. 18).

The Jews are extremely divided in Paul's day, and these Roman Jews reply that they had not received letters from Judea, nor had they heard anything evil against Paul. The rumors are about Paul in Judea have not spread, but the gospel has. The Jewish leadership in Rome has heard about the Way but do not have a face to go with the message they've heard. Now they do.

Paul's example reminds us of the importance of presentation. The face of Christianity affects nonbelievers' perceptions. Christianity operates best on a 1:1 and 1:2 basis. When you introduce faith into a conversation, people often say, "I did not perceive it to be this way."

For example, after an interfaith event held at our church, one of our guests told me about her journey to the church. She said, "Before I came,

I did not know much about you Baptists, but I did know one person here. If that person was anything like Jesus, then I wanted to follow that person because that would mean following Jesus."

The face you give to faith is so critical to conversion. The Jewish people in Rome had heard a lot about Christians, now they wanted to talk.

Understand the Challenge (28:23-28)

Acts explains why the gospel is so challenging to Paul. Not everyone who hears it receives it. Paul finds the answer from an ancient text that validates his current experience, paraphrasing Isaiah 6:9-10, which most Jewish people would have known (vv. 25-27). Paul applies the verses to his circumstances in Acts, and by extension we can also apply it to our experiences sharing the gospel. Most Christians have also heard this parable earlier in Luke's Gospel. Jesus uses Isaiah 6:9-10 in his parable of the sower and the seed to explain why people reject his message. When some people hear Paul's message, they become hard-hearted, a prominent reaction throughout scripture. For instance, in Pharaoh's response to Moses, sometimes Pharaoh hardens his heart; at others God hardens Pharaoh's. Based on my experience, hardening the heart can have both negative and positive effects. Sometimes it's a sign of outright rejection; at others, it's the beginning of openness.

A person can reject the gospel out of stubbornness. Think of it like a person chewing an old piece of gum or gristle in steak. After awhile, what is soft and tasty becomes brittle and hard if all the person does is chew. The longer one spends challenging the gospel, the less likely the person is to receive it.

Hardness of heart can also have a positive effect on someone, especially during times of struggle. Someone might reject the message initially because they are offended, and later turn toward Christ. This response happens in athletic training. A coach will "toughen up" a soft offensive lineman on a football team to get him to play his position with more intensity. A kid may show up to training camp out of shape needing to stretch, run, and work out in order to perform for the team. He may not like the commands from the coach (and neither do the parents); but if he sticks with the program, he can play the game.

When my son Parker played peewee football, the league limited the size of receivers, quarterbacks, and running backs due to safety concerns. Several of the boys were too big to touch the ball. Coaches put them on the offensive line. When they practiced with these boys, however, they would not block or hit anyone. The smallest guys would run right past or over them. The taller fourth graders usually had younger siblings and had been told their entire lives *not* to push anyone because they were bigger than the average kid. Once on the field, when told to go out and hit someone, they could not make themselves do so. The coaches had to find ways to upset them so that they could learn to play their position.

The gospel doesn't find the meanness in us; it finds the goodness in us. When the ball of life comes our way, the gospel confronts us and says, "You have to go to these people." Paul experienced both rejection and reception when he preached. As the people rejected him, their responses only advanced the gospel.

Paul's paraphrase of Isaiah 6:9-10 illustrates how one response to the gospel builds on another (vv. 26-27). This is an ancient rhetorical technique called an *antithesis*, where one statement has the effect of building upon another. Think of these verses like steps working from the bottom up. The goal that Paul expresses is for God to heal the people; at first, the people reject. However, each pair builds on the others. Each one is a contrast.

> and I would heal them. (Acts 28:26-27)
> and listen with their ears,
> and understand with their heart and turn—
> and they have shut their eyes;
> so that they might not look with their eyes
> and their ears are hard of hearing,
> For this people's heart has grown dull,
> and you will indeed look, but never perceive.
> You will indeed listen, but never understand,

For those who share the gospel, the good news is that we are not responsible for others' reactions. We are responsible for sharing the message. Sometimes rejection is the first sign of eventual acceptance. Success can't only be measured by who "gets it" or who comes to hear the message. Rejection can be a sign that the message is going forth.

If our responsibility is to share and go, then something happens to us in the going. We are changed by the unhindered gospel.

Changed by the Unhindered Gospel (28:29-31)

As in Acts 20, Paul works with his own hands, welcoming all who come to him and teaching about the Lord Jesus Christ with all boldness and without hindrance. The word in Greek literally translates "unhinderedly." We do not have an English equivalent for this expression.

The gospel has been going forth, breaking down barriers, and as it goes, it does three very important things.[1]

1. Philanthropy

As Paul welcomes us in Acts, he shows us what true philanthropy is. On Malta, the non-Christian Publius shares out of the abundance of his heart with no strings attached. He gives to Paul without the promise of a tax benefit, public recognition, or a gift in return. In our world, even philanthropy is all about the giver instead of the recipient. Church is one of the last places where we have the chance to give anonymously to avoid creating an expectation of control or power on the part of the giver. In Acts, philanthropy is unconditional. They do not worry about the giver.

2. Friendship

The community of the church forms a common bond of friendship where individuals share everything. If I were to ask you, "When was the last time someone other than your immediate family took something from your closet? And you freely gave it to them, no questions asked? And they never returned it? And you didn't worry about it?" That's difficult to do in the South. In my family of origin, we may not be able to remember where we left our keys or our computer passwords, but we are taught early on to remember who took what from us. We live in a world of private ownership; everything I have is mine. "What's mine is mine. If I want you to use it, you can, but you better use it correctly." With the friends we have as Christians, we can share freely.

3. Hospitality

Strangers are not only expected but welcomed when they arrive. Paul has an open-door policy with strangers. The guests shape the gospel as it moves out.

How do you finish the story? Usually, we add the ending that sounds most logical. Most people think Acts ends with Paul's beheading and Peter's crucifixion, neither of which are detailed in the Bible at all. Rather, the story of Acts is written by every succeeding generation that believes the message. We are the ones who finish the story. We are Acts 29–30. We are the ones who practice philanthropy, friendship, and hospitality offered "unhinderedly."

NOTE

1. Mikeal C. Parsons, *Acts*, Paideia Commentaries on the New Testament (Grand Rapids: Baker Academic, 2008), 367.